The Bible as a whole is a story, a grand narrative, that grips our hearts, our minds, our imaginations. We join with Jesus and His community on a quest which demands our best effort in the team's mission. The end is glorious indeed. *The Stories We Live* is a great introduction to that grand narrative and also some of the broken stories which distract many. Read, be gripped by the story, and join the quest!

–GERRY BRESHEARS,
Professor of Theology,
Western Seminary, Portland.

THE STORIES WE LIVE

Discovering the True and Better Way of Jesus.

SEAN POST

Foreword by RICK MCKINLEY

THE STORIES WE LIVE

Discovering the True and Better Way of Jesus

SEAN POST

GCD BOOKS

To Melissa,

I'm grateful for the story we share together.

TABLE OF CONTENTS

FOREWORD

Great stories affect all of us. The words "once upon a time" continue to spark the interest of our imagination even after our childhood has faded. I am glad that Sean has written this book. Having known him for many years, I have grown to appreciate his ability to tie together the deep affections of the heart and the deep thoughts of the mind. He offers us an invitation to a better story.

Today we are all seeking a better story to live into. Often times the ancient story of Scripture is dismissed for what we deem a more compelling story—one of becoming our own hero. Yet as hard as we try our own brokenness keeps creeping up and rewriting our efforts into a deeper isolation and sense of meaninglessness.

At the center of our longings there's an inescapable desire for something larger, something more, something loving and creative and beautiful, but that something is always beyond our reach. When we turn to the church many people seem are disappointed in the story that she is telling. A reduced religious prescription of how to be good and nice leaves the heart longing for the mystery and beauty and narrative of the Jesus life that is all but hidden in the rules and regulations that seem to fall from the lips of our pulpits.

In The Stories We Live, Sean captures both the imagination and mystery and grandness of the story we find ourselves in. He pulls back the curtain on the main Author of the world's drama our Trinitarian God—the Father, Son, and Spirit.

This is the type of book the people of God need so desperately today. He takes the questions of the culture and connects them to the foundation of Christians theology. As a good missionary, Sean listens to the story of the Scripture to discover the redemptive answers our hearts have always longed for and continue to long for. In the Bible we find the love story that is filled with passion, meaning, and heaven on earth.

By engaging culture Sean helps us to understand where our deepest questions are coming from, how we got to this moment we find ourselves in, and brings us deep insight into the longings and mystery's that effect believer and skeptic alike.

By engaging scripture and theology Sean points to a better story that does not side step the difficult questions or reduce things down to trite answers, but instead opens up for us a majestic and hopeful journey into a deeper story of holy love.

My prayer is that as you read this book, you will find a rock onto which to build your life and fall in love with your Lover that is our God.

RICK MCKINLEY
Lead Pastor, Imago Dei Community

INTRODUCTION

If your life were a movie, would anyone buy tickets to watch? Would you?

The question provokes thought because most of the time we lack the perspective to see our lives as a story. Of course, the credits aren't rolling on your story yet. You have more life to live. But what kind of story will you live?

I've always been astounded by the audacity of Everest climbers. If they weren't so well prepared we might mistake them as reckless. But each one has counted the cost of the expedition. Each one has paid a steep price for the opportunity to sweat and stagger breathlessly towards the highest point on earth. For reasons known only to themselves, they aim for the summit carried forward by desire that astounds us.

Like those climbers, you and I are in the middle of an expedition. Are you aware of what "summit" you are journeying towards? Have you considered what it is you are chasing? What are the desires you are trading your life for?

I'm not sure there are any questions more important than these. They require deep self-awareness. Yet none of us knows ourselves perfectly. Our self-knowledge is limited. So what if you invited God into this conversation? The Bible says that his Spirit can reveal to us the secrets of our own heart. If you are interested in exploring this kind of truth, I'm confident God is willing join you in the process.

THE AIM OF THIS BOOK

Being human means you are in the middle of a story war. There is a dangerous riptide of broken stories that threaten to pull you away from the invitation of Jesus.

This book is about charting those tides. But even more than that, it's about being rescued from their grasp. As you move through the book, each chapter is titled a "conversation." My deep hope is that the ideas of each conversation will be something you process with others. That's why the end of each conversation includes reflective questions that address your head, your heart, and your hands. I've gone with the labels "Think," "Love," and "Do" to help you understand the trajectory of each question.

By the time you're finished, you will understand the universal framework that composes the stories we live. You will also be able to map the components of your story and identify the false loves you pursue and how those stories are broken so that you can live into the true and better story of God.

LIFE AS A HOUSE

The film *Life as a House* opens with a stunning panorama of the Southern California coastline. We see the sun rise as it peeks over the cliffs and you can hear the waves crashing below. The camera pans and we are introduced to the main character who is facing the ocean, stretching, and urinating off the cliff.

George Monroe is the owner of this magnificent property and his neighbors hate him for it. Surrounded by pristine mansions, his embarrassing shack is in disrepair (and no functioning toilet, thus, the need for the cliff). The great irony is that George is an architect. However, he hates his job. He is divorced and alienated from his drug-loving son.

Early on in the movie, George collapses after being fired. Doctors discover he has terminal cancer. Mere months remain in his life. With the end in view, he sets to work on the project he's always dreamed of—pouring his energy and skill into his house. He enlists the help of his son Sam who violently opposes the idea but is forced to help by his mother. Sam moves in for the summer.

George has not shared the news of his cancer with anyone, but as his condition worsens the secret leaks. Sam begins to soften towards his father. As the cancer slowly kills George, his house is being constructed and repaired. But even better, a relationship between George and Sam blossoms out of the rubble.

As summer fades, George is hospitalized and it is clear that his death is imminent. Sam places Christmas lights on the house, so George can see it from a distance in his hospital room.

George dies. The building is finished. The movie ends with a voice-over of his final words to Sam.

> I always thought of myself as a house. I was always what I lived in. It didn't need to be big; it didn't even need to be beautiful; it just needed to be mine. I became what I was meant to be. I built myself a life. . . . I built myself a house. . . . If you were a house, Sam, this is where you would want to be built: on rock, facing the sea. Listening. Listening.[1]

For you and I, the credits aren't rolling. You and I can still build. You are, in fact, building something with your life right now. It's the story you live.

---

[1] "Life as a House (2001) – Quotes – Imdb," IMDb. Accessed April 17, 2015. http://www.imdb.com/title/tt0264796/quotes

THE STORIES WE LIVE
Conversation 1

What is it about stories that captivate us? At the end of a long day, what compels you to sit down and watch an episode of your favorite TV show? When we imbibe a story well told its enjoyable and intoxicating because for a moment we taste a different reality.

We are hardwired for story. All our songs tell stories. We pay billions of dollars each year to lose ourselves for a couple hours in the plots Hollywood trades for our cash. But for all the benefits of our entertainment, there is a lethal downside. We get drunk on the stories others tell while failing to attend to the story we are living. (Perhaps in some way that's how the phrase "binge-watching" was coined.) Big budget movies, romance novels, video games, and celebrity gossip can numb us to the adventure we have actually been invited to participate in.

I was recently backpacking with some young men in the Cascade Mountains. With no cell service, no Wi-Fi, and no technology to distract I was eager to connect with these guys. At the end of the day, we sat down around the fire and the conversation commenced. One discussion unfolded with particular enthusiasm and debate. The topic was video games. The guys talked about maps, weapons, skills, and killing dragons. I should've told them, "You are already on a map. You are a character with unique skills. And you are already in the middle of an adventure so much more real than that game you paid fifty bucks for."

Stories are how we know. Some philosophers have put it this way: "Narrative is epistemology." Epistemology is the branch of philosophy that deals with how we know what we know. Everything that can be known—from how to change a diaper to why you should vote for a particular political party—comes to us preaching some story about the way things have been, the way things are, and the way things ought to be.

Stories are vital to our makeup because they are the frequency by which we make sense of the world. The Greeks were curious, "Where did fire come from?" They answered their own question with a story, "Prometheus stole it from the gods." The Greeks crafted some fascinating myths in an effort to understand their origins and why the world was the way it was.

But stories do even more than help us make sense of the world. They actually chart the meaning for our lives. What we know sets the trajectory for how we live. We actually begin to inhabit the stories we tell.

For example, the Dreamworks film *The Croods* imagines the lives of a prehistoric family. The family's two children are raised by a protective father who explains the world to them as dangerous and deadly. As a result, they spend almost all their time in a dark cave to stay safe. The father's narrative (a dangerous and deadly world) informs their practices and rhythms as a family (live in the cave to minimize risk).

IDENTIFYING YOUR STORY

If the story you tell about the world becomes the story you live, then life's most important question is, "What story am I living?" The most meaningful task you could ever undertake is to bring your story under the lights for interrogation. After all, this story shapes your decisions, informs your emotions, forms your habits, and determines your values and vision. So summon this narrative to the interrogation room and ask, "Are you true? Are you worth it?" But to honestly interrogate your story, you must interrogate yourself.

This is a challenge because we often lie to ourselves to protect sentimentality, relationships, and priorities. So how can one overcome the propensity towards self-deception and lack of awareness? A great first step in the process is to realize that at their core, all stories are really the same.

All stories are the same because every story's plot must address certain unavoidable questions. The story you believe involves beginnings. It's a story that involves brokenness and pain. It's a story of redemption and rescue. It is a story that offers hope for restoration. You might call this story your "good news" or your "gospel" (the terms are synonymous).

Beginnings

The four-year old who asks mom, "Where do babies come from?" is asking questions about the origin of their personhood. Of course, once we're old enough to learn about storks and how the stork dropped us off at our parent's house . . . that was how we got my two sons anyway. The point is we cannot avoid inquiring about our beginnings.

Ted Ward writes, "Why is a very human question. When you ask it, you are making an important claim on being a person. Why shows belief in purpose. Why says that you want to share anything that anyone else knows about what lies beyond the obvious. Why shows self-respect: you believe that you are capable of understanding."[2]

You might say that "beginnings" is the pivotal introduction to the purpose and design of everything in any story. Even worldviews that believe human existence is purposeless still answer the "Why?" question of purpose.

Brokenness

What is wrong with the world? Ask a million people and you'll get a few thousand answers. On a macro-level some might say, "We are destroying our planet with careless environmental practices." Or, "The Christian values of our forefathers have eroded into a corrupt government." On a smaller scale, some-

---

[2] Ted Ward. *Values Begin at Home.* Wheaton, IL: Victor Books, 1989. 85.

one might say, "My dad walked out on us. That's why my whole family is so messed up."

There's a lot of pain and suffering in our world. There's a lot that is broken both in our individual lives and on a global scale. How does the story you have aligned your life with account for that pain and suffering? How are we to make sense of the brokenness that attaches itself to our lives like a parasite?

Redemption

The word "redeem" means to buy back. Redemption is part of the framework for everyone's meta-narrative because we're all looking to be delivered from something and brought into something else. As a result, everyone trusts a functional savior.

- "Money will deliver me from instability and uncertainty and offer me security."
- "This relationship will deliver me from loneliness and give me intimacy."
- "Entertainment will deliver me from boredom and offer me escape from _____."

We place our faith in these redeemers to save us from our brokenness then to make things right in the end. That's the final part of the framework.

Restoration

This is the "happily ever after" part of the story we know so well from fairy tales. The story you are living has an ideal end. Some kind of vision of the way things ought to be. Maybe your picture-perfect ending involves a large house with lots of toys. Maybe you imagine a future where everyone takes better care of the environment and legislation adequately enforces that stewardship. Perhaps your vision of restoration is marked by intimate romance.

In your mind, when everything is as it should be, what will the world look like? When your redeeming savior has done what you trust it to do, what does life look like for you and for others?

THE SHAPE OF A STORY

In the 1980's Disney began using a very intentional strategy to write their movies. Honey I Shrunk the Kids, The Little Mermaid, Beauty and the Beast, Aladdin, The Lion King, and Toy Story were all products of some simple story patterns.[3]

In 1949, Joseph Campbell published *The Hero With a Thousand Faces*. After studying hundreds of myths from all over the world, Campbell identified remarkable parallels within those epics. In the 1980's, Disney began using Campbell's ideas to help write their stories. Screenwriter Christopher Vogler then wrote *The Writer's Journey* where he distills Campbell's ideas on the hero myth into twelve stages. These stages were then used to help write the aforementioned Disney hits.

- **Ordinary World**: he hero's normal world before the story begins
- **Call to Adventure:** The hero is presented with a problem, challenge, or adventure
- **Refusal of the Call:** The hero refuses the challenge or journey, usually because he's scared or wounded by previous experiences in some way
- **Meeting with the Mentor:** The hero meets a mentor to gain advice or training for the adventure
- **Crossing the First Threshold:** The hero leaves the Ordinary World and goes into the Special World
- **Tests, Allies, Enemies:** the hero faces tests, meets allies, confronts enemies, and learns the rules of the Special World
- **Approach:** The hero has hit setbacks during tests and may need to try a new idea
- **Ordeal:** The biggest life-or-death crisis
- **Reward:** The hero has survived death, overcomes his fear, and now earns the reward

---

[3] Michael Frost and Alan Hirsch, *The Faith of Leap*. Grand Rapids, MI: Baker Books, 2011. 107.

- **The Road Back:** The hero must return to the Ordinary World
- **Resurrection Hero:** Another test where the hero faces death—he has to use everything he's learned
- **Return with Elixir:** The hero returns from the journey with the "elixir," and uses it to help everyone in the Ordinary World[4]

Although you probably don't have the twelve stages of the hero myth memorized, you do recognize it. You could watch *Fight Club* or *Cinderella* and see how both films follow this same strategy. What is somewhat surprising is that we never tire of this story. We only groan when it is presented poorly. If the stages are presented well, we are more than happy to continue consuming beautifully woven stories.

How can this be? How can we never tire of narratives that tread this well-worn path? Perhaps because in some way the hero-myth is the way we would like things to be in our life and in our world.

Whether or not we realize it, the hero myth is the way things actually are. Right now, you are in the middle of a pursuit driven by love. You might be in love with the ideal of a new sports car and you face tests, allies, and enemies in pursuit of that love. You might be in love with achievement and the reward that could be yours.

Maybe the most superficial—yet enlightening—question we could ask to begin the interrogation of the story you are living is this: "If Disney turned my story into a movie, would I buy a ticket to watch it? Would anyone else?"

EVERY STORY IS A LOVE STORY

One of my favorite films is *There Will Be Blood*, starring Daniel Day Lewis. Lewis plays the role of Daniel Plainview, an 1890's oil prospector. Through incredible risk and danger, Plainview

---

4 ibid.

slowly builds an oil business and hires employees. One day, an on-the-job accident kills a worker—who is the father of an infant. Plainview adopts this boy as his own and calls him H.W. The film fast-forwards a dozen years. We are re-introduced to Plainview as both a single father and a successful oil tycoon. From there the story unfolds. The movie is nothing less than a love story. More specifically, it is a story of two great loves in conflict with one another: the love the father has for a son and the love the same man has for money. The tension of the film is the question, "Which love will win out?"

The awakening of love and desire is secret ingredient that drives every great story. In a moment a spark ignites within a rather ordinary person and sets them on an adventure. The moment "The Eye of the Tiger" starts in and Rocky begins training with inspiring tenacity. Depending on which *Rocky* you watch he's either fighting to prove his self-worth, fighting for his family, or fighting to avenge a friend. The greatest stories are when a noble desire drives a worthy quest.

Your story is fundamentally a story of desire. This is true because we are desiring beings. That is what it means to be human.

The rallying cry for the Enlightenment was Rene Descartes' epiphany, "I think, therefore I am." This declaration birthed a school of thought called "rationalism," which considered a person to be primarily defined by their thinking. Thus the conclusion, "Humans are primarily thinking beings." But are we really nothing more than walking brains? Does our humanity consist primarily in the efficiency of our neural pathways?

Most often our lives are not lived by what we know so much as they are by what we crave and long for. In other words, we rarely behave based on what we know. More frequently we behave and decide based on what we desire.

This truth explains why it is so hard to talk someone out of an abusive relationship. Even when you present them with the reality of their abuse, they overlook it in exchange for what they really want: the relationship and whatever it symbolizes. Or consider someone who knows her bad eating habits are endangering her health—but doesn't stop. Clearly, what we know is not as defining as what we want. James K.A. Smith writes,

> To be human is to love, and it is what we love that defines who we are. Our [ultimate] love is constitutive of our identity. . . . Our ultimate love is what we worship."[5] He moves on to explain that by necessity every love is attached to a particular *telos* or goal: "In other words, what we love is a specific vision of the good life, an implicit picture of what we think human flourishing looks like. . . . Our ultimate love moves and motivates us because we are lured by this picture of human flourishing.[6]

So what is the ultimate love your story centers on? Are you able to identify it? That love is the pivot point of the story you are living.

FOUR THEMES BURIED IN EVERY PLOT

Every story is a love story, but the stories we live also contain other themes. The way we allow these themes to play out in our lives is an important part of examining our story. Douglas John Hall describes four common themes or "quests" we pursue: moral authenticity, meaningful community, transcendence and mystery, and meaning.[7]

Theme #1: To Be Good

Arete is a Greek word and is synonymous with the concept of excellence. Greek philosophers use this word to describe the state of an object that has fulfilled its purpose. Microwaves are

---

[5] James K.A. Smith. *Desiring the Kingdom.* Grand Rapids, MI: Baker Academic, 2009. 51-52.

[6] ibid.

[7] George Hunsberger and Craig Van Gelder. *The Church between Gospel and Culture.* Grand Rapids, MI: William B. Eerdmans Publishing Co., 1996. 207.

excellent when they perform according to their function—heating up frozen food or leftovers. Whales are excellent when they find all the food they need to stay alive and then reproduce themselves and take care of their offspring. But what makes an excellent human being? What would it mean for a human to fulfill his or her purpose for existence?

Although it is tempting to ignore these challenging questions, it is also impossible to move through life without in some sense answering them. These questions touch upon the "beginnings" portion of your story.

Even if you cannot comprehensively answer what it means to be an excellent human, you would probably be very confident in describing what it means to be a poor human being. If we sat down to talk, you could conjure up all sorts of negative examples of how particular people act in ways that are harmful to themselves and/or harmful to humanity.

Cultural anthropologists have discovered almost universal moral principles adhered to in nearly every cultural context. In the vast majority of the world, murder is considered to be detrimental to society. An individual in a highly populated urban context and an individual from a remote tribal context will almost certainly agree that killing another human is a departure from what ought to be. Such an action does not constitute excellence in what it means to be human.

During my senior year of high school, I remember being interviewed by a local newspaper for a piece they were doing on graduates who had outstanding records of community service. Somehow the service hours I had accumulated during detention counted so I was to be a recipient of this service award. The reporter asked what I would like to be said of me when I died. I quickly replied, "I want people to say that I lived life to the fullest." The reporter interjected and called for a timeout in the interview. She asked me to reconsider my answer on the grounds that it was the same answer every single interviewee had given.

When someone says, "I want to live life to the fullest," the essence of what they are expressing is a desire to be fully human. Whatever it means to be human we don't want to miss out on it. Because this desire and this fear are so prevalent, we will necessarily piece together some sort of definition and under-standing of what it means to be an excellent human being. Even if that definition is nothing more than a negation and avoidance of the evils we see in the world around us.

Theme #2: Authentic Community

For the vast majority of us, "community" is a word that is still awaiting content. We crave it, but have never quite experienced it as we hoped it would be. Perhaps for a short time we did, but then it proved to be a lie and a let down. Or perhaps in our cynicism and skepticism—and even a little bitterness—we have subdued this desire for fear that it cannot be fulfilled anyhow.

Almost more than any other culture in history, Western so-ciety is characterized by a heightened sense of individualism. Children of the West like to think of themselves as autonomous. We go to great lengths to make ourselves financially independ-ent and secure so that we will not have to rely on others. We coined the phrases "self-made man" and "self-made woman." When our individualism collides with our innate craving for community the only sort of community that our individualism will allow is a superficial socialization that aims only to further our personal autonomy and independence. "Community is only good in so far as it helps my personal bottom-line and profit-ability." That sort of "community" is not satisfying for anyone.

In the stirring film *Into the Wild*, Chris McCandless aban-dons the affluence and security of his family and sets out on a journey to explore, to push his personal boundaries, and to ex-perience a different kind of life. Chris runs into other charac-ters along this journey, but his interactions with them are sim-ply side notes in the story of his personal journey. This explora-tion ends in the mountains of Alaska. Alone Chris makes his home an old abandoned bus. He is both befriended and con-quered by the wildness of nature. But the victory is short-lived. In the last moments of his life, as his soul slips from his body he experiences an epiphany that surely would've altered the jour-ney he had taken. "Happiness is only real when shared."

Stories like *Into the Wild* may carry little appeal for you. You're on the other side of the spectrum. Instead of being captured by "lone wolf" stories you imagine a human utopia. In this relational paradise, everyone treats others as they ought to be treated and as they would like to be treated. This community is the epitome of love, unity, and togetherness. People care for each other, take care of each other, and meet each other's needs. Over and over you've tried to create a web of relationships like this. But it has never come to fruition. The project is always sabotaged either by your own shortcomings or others not taking your community project seriously. You've begun to wonder if real community is possible.

Theme #3: Transcendence and Mystery

The word "transcend" means to surpass and go beyond. As humans, this is the sense that "there must be something more than what I'm experiencing" and "there's got to be more to it than what I know." When something is transcendent it defies physical boundaries and limitations of knowledge or experience.

We all tend to gravitate towards and appreciate experiences and moments that are larger than ourselves. Why do hundreds of thousands of fans crowd city streets each year for Super Bowl parades? They want to be part of the team. They know the team is much bigger than their individual self.

Why is there a universal appreciation for nature and its breathtaking scenery? It reminds us that we exist in a universe that is much bigger than ourselves.

At a core level we understand that if there is not something larger and more surpassing then our imperfect existence than life is not worth living. People fill this desire for transcendence in different ways—and not necessarily through belief in a higher power.

How does this desire for transcendence play out? Tim Keller identifies one gigantic outlet of choice. He suggests that our culture has front-loaded its desire for transcendence into romance and love.[8] In Western society, it seems we have higher expectations for intimacy within romance then in any other time or culture. Our hope for participation in transcendence expresses itself—for many—in their romantic outlets in the expectations they place upon those relationships.

Other individuals look to drugs or other substances that can provide release to their mind. Depending on the drug, some highs become a euphoric experience that users would say isn't possible otherwise.

Theme #4: Meaning

We all want to feel that the stories we live are of value because they express some kind of truth. We want to believe that there is a beauty and goodness and a richness we have contributed to the world through our story.

On the football field, teams succeed when they move the ball into the end zone, putting six points on the board. Without the goal the drive means nothing. Without the end zone, it's not worth the risk of injury, the blood, the sweat, and the energy. The hope of a touchdown actually brings purpose and energy to the offensive players. The players sense meaning in what they're doing right now. Every action either contributes to or detracts from the goal.

In a similar sense, our lives are inevitably building towards a goal. Every thought, action, and human interaction finds significance only so far as it is connected to our ultimate sense of meaning and purpose.

Imagine you have a friend who's only purpose is to build a seven-figure bank account so that they can entertain themselves and feel a sense of fun and security. That's their personal "end zone." For them, meaning is contributing to that goal. Every conversation, decision, and relationship is only useful in so far as it feeds that purpose and continues the "drive." The same is true of anyone in their pursuit of meaning.

---

[8] ibid, 60.

"All over the western world there are covert and overt attempts to discover purpose – not a purpose we ourselves invent, but a horizon of meaning towards which we may turn. As Kurt Vonnegut says one way or another in all of his strange and wonderful novels, perhaps cynically or perhaps seriously, purposeless things are abhorrent to the human species; and if the human species suspects that it is it self purposeless it becomes conspicuously suicidal."[9]

Philosopher, Albert Camus expressed a similar sentiment, "The silence of the universe has led me to conclude that the world is without meaning." The utter emptiness of the universe is a chief tenet of the nihilistic school of thought. "Yet Camus was not content to remain a nihilist. He fought to transcend it, to make meaning where there was none."[10]

During a private dialogue with pastor, Howard Mumma, Camus said, "I am searching for something I do not have, something I'm not sure I can define. . . . The world is not rational, it does not fit human needs and desire. In a word, our very existence is absurd. Suicide seems the only logical response."[11]

The difficulty of our technological age is that we have the ability to substitute entertainment for meaning. We can find ourselves caught up in the stories produced and fine-tuned by Hollywood. And in the moments we are not able to watch those stories on the TV, we find ourselves bored with our own lives. This boredom is a troubling symptom that deserves our sincere attention. It is indicative of a discontent with our own lives and a desire to be somewhere else, doing something else. This state of being indicates that we have not yet laid a hold of a true sense of meaning and purpose. When we possess purpose we find that simple tasks like changing diapers, paying taxes, and waking up in the morning actually connect to that overarching

---

[9] ibid, 212.

[10] Tullian Tchividjian. *Glorious Ruin*. Colorado Springs, CO: David C. Cook, 2012. 115.

[11] James W. Sire, "Camus the Christian?." *Christianity Today*. October 23, 2000. Accessed April 17, 2015. http://www.christianitytoday.com/ct/2000/october23/39.121.html.

meaning. We begin to sense that even the most mundane moments of our lives are building to something significant.

REFLECTING ON THE STORY THAT DRIVES YOUR LIFE

As we've discussed, everyone's life is shaped by an overarching story we place our trust in. This is our personal "good news." Our identity is actually wrapped up in this narrative because the narrative teaches us what to desire and then leads us deeper into that desire.

Now is your chance to think about this story. These reflections are intended to drive you to clarify what you're placing your faith in to deliver you from both internal and external brokenness and effect redemption and restoration.

If you've ever made a commitment to heighten your physical fitness, you know success is more likely with a workout partner. The same principle holds true as you engage the process of identifying your story. You may be more successful if you approach these questions conversationally with at least one other person. That way, there's no easy way of escaping the self-discovery that these questions are crafted to produce.

THINK

- How would you explain your "good news"?
- What is the supreme desire or quest that fuels your life?

LOVE

- If you could choose your ultimate love, would it be the same or different than the ultimate love that currently drives your life?
- If you could change what you wanted most in life, what would it be, and why?

DO

- Ask a friend or family member about their "good news" story using beginnings, brokenness, redemption, and restoration questions. Ask their permission to share what you are discovering about the narrative that is directing your life.

THE TRUE AND BETTER STORY
Conversation 2

I clipped the buckles and tightened the straps on my son's re-straining device. It was a car seat not a straight jacket. I admit they are similar in their usefulness when parenting small chil-dren. We drove for a half hour and jib-jabbed about cars and trucks and helicopters and mommy.

The first time we visited Snoqualmie Falls was a few months earlier. We looked over the viewing deck as it was snowing lightly. A harsh wind sucked the heat right off our faces.

This time around the sun was out—restoring my faith in its existence as a Pacific Northwesterner. We paused and stared in the exact spot where my son cried from the cold before. This time around, he was mesmerized. Mist tickled our faces as the falls pounded the river hundreds of feet below. I started won-dering how that first drop of water dripped over the falls . . .

Have you ever wondered what kick-started life? Of course, theories abound about our origins. The Bible says that life came from life.

BEGINNINGS

Imagine with me.

The earth is desolate and void. But a community of love, to-getherness, and goodness "is." God the Father, God the Son, and God the Spirit have always existed together in this perfect community. They have never not been one unified essence, three distinct, harmonious, co-equal persons.

Now this Triune God does something that we would not expect yet is perfectly true to His essence. He reaches outside of the perfect community of himself to create. Everything is good. But he creates man and woman. He says they are "very good."

The clue as to why humans are "very good" is wrapped up in the special language God used to create them. He said, "Let us make man in our image, after our likeness." So man was created in the image of the Creator. Among all God created, they had the unique ability to display God's character. They had the unique responsibility to reflect his nature and to overflow with the beauty of his character. This shared way of being created common ground for communication and relationship with God.

After God creates, he relates with Adam and Eve face to face. In the Garden Eden, God enjoys morning walks with them. God converses with Adam and Eve as they grow in their understanding. God explores his creation with them. God plays and recreates with them. God works on projects and builds stuff with them.

God's directive to Adam and Eve was to cultivate the untamed land. He made the world out of nothing. Then He commanded humans to make something out of what he had made. Adam and Eve were created to create. To make something of the world that God had made and entrusted to them.

BROKENNESS

One day, a crafty serpent tempts Eve to "become like God" by eating forbidden fruit. Eve eats. Adam eats. Satan's lie is that there was a way of being which was better than what God had already declared "very good." The clear implication is, "What God called very good is not actually the greatest good available to you. There is a greater good which God is withholding from you."

In seeking to become something other than what they are, Adam and Eve forsake their friendship with God. Goodness and wholeness are replaced with perversion and brokenness. As overseers of creation, the curse of their sin trickles down into nature. The tragedy of brokenness not only strikes nature but becomes an inherited disease within the human heart from the moment of conception.

Adam and Eve don't enjoy walking with God anymore. Upon discovering their own nakedness, they hide from him in shame. With sadness in his voice, God invites confession, "Adam, where are you?" After a conversation filled with refusal to accept personal responsibility for their sin God responds to their rebellion.

God responds to their rebellion with blood. God doesn't take Adam and Eve's blood. He sacrifices an animal and uses the skin to cover their nakedness and their shame. He removes them from the Garden, but not without good news. One day, the offspring of Woman will crush the head of the serpent. But first the serpent would deliver a blow to this offspring's heel. Somehow God was plotting to redeem. Within minutes of the rebellion, the Trinity begins to enact a lengthy, costly, and risky mission of redemption and restoration.

Within one generation, man has now moved from being with God face-to-face to killing fellow image-bearers of God. After several generations, earth has become utterly wicked except for one family. God's emotional response to evil is grief and anger. God delivers Noah and his family from a flood of judgment he brings on the earth then establishes a covenant with him.

A few generations later, God establishes a promise with a man named Abraham. His purpose is to begin to create a new humanity from within humanity—a people that belong to him and his purposes for the world.

Through doubt, struggle, and scandal, Abraham's family multiplies and came to be known as "Israel." But God also told Abraham his descendants would be enslaved for four hundred years. During this time, other nations inhabit the land God had promised to Israel. These nations grew more and more powerful although they sacrificed their children to idols and practiced heinous sexual rituals.

In their suffering and enslavement, Israel cries out. God listens with compassion to the oppression of his people and selects a leader named Moses to serve as his mouthpiece. God prepares to deliver his people from bondage. After a series of miracles and judgments against the Egyptian pharaoh—who refuses to respond to his warnings—God brings Israel through the Red Sea and single-handedly destroys their enemies who are in pursuit.

Israel is unable to fulfill the Abrahamic covenant by loving God, trusting God, and worshipping God. So in order to provide a picture of what this looks like, God gives them Ten Commandments to carefully obey.

Israel also refuses to trust in God's promise to give them the land. They are fixated on the strength of the other nations and their own weakness, rather than focusing in on the promise of God. They are forced to wander in the wilderness for 40 years. Then Moses dies and God raises up Joshua to lead the people into the land. Under Joshua's lead, God drives out the nations from the Promised Land.

The other laws given to the people via Moses become a central means for spotlighting the evil of the human heart. Although the laws themselves are good, Israel made the mistake of either neglecting the law entirely, or using the law in such a way that it's true purpose was lost.

After hundreds of years of anarchy, oppression, evil kings, and a divided Kingdom, Judah (the southern kingdom of Israel) was taken into captivity. Everything about God's promises seemed dead, but God raised up prophetic voices to speak to his people before, during, and after the Babylonian exile.

The prophets lived in a time when it seemed that all God's promises to Israel could never be fulfilled due to Israel's disobedience. But through God's Spirit, they foretold a time when a Suffering Servant would come to pay the penalty for sin. This Messiah would be the messenger of a new covenant.

REDEMPTION

The Son, Jesus, is a card-carrying member of the Trinity. The Son shares the same divine essence as the Father and the Spirit. The Son possesses all of the attributes of God. Of course there are incommunicable attributes of God that humans can never share. Things like being all-knowing, all-powerful, everywhere-present, self-existent, and self-sufficient. The Son possesses these. There are also communicable attributes of God. Qualities that humans are designed to share with God. Things like goodness, mercy, love, and justice. The Son possesses these too.

But now God's ongoing restorative mission reaches a new and unpredictably daring climax. The Father, the Son, and the Holy Spirit partner together to remove a member of the Trinity from heaven! The Son leaves heaven.

And the Son does not leave heaven with the incommunicable and infinite power of God in his pocket. No. In complete vulnerability the Son becomes fully human. He surrenders independent exercise of his divine attributes and exchanges them to live a perfectly Spirit-filled and Father-dependent life.

Although the Son is God, he comes to the world not holding to his rights as God, but actually surrendering them. He is naked in a metaphorical sense. And in a literal sense too. If this story could even be more risky—the eternal, infinite, invisible Creator breaks into human history as a naked, crying, defenseless baby.

The Son cannot feed himself. He cannot protect himself from King Herod who is seeking to murder all boys under age two. He cannot clothe himself. He cannot keep himself warm. He cannot provide for himself. He cannot even communicate besides using different modes of crying to relay his needs to the imperfect parents to which he has entrusted himself. But God the Father protects the Son by sending an angel to warn the parents to go to Egypt until the mayhem is complete.

Jesus grows as a human in wisdom. Physically. Socially. He learns. He experiences fatigue, slept, grew hungry, and thirst. He learns a trade and works as a carpenter. He probably smashes his thumb with tools on occasion and probably isn't the best carpenter or the worst. The Son has friends. He loves kids, celebrates holidays, goes to parties, experiences grief and anxiety. The Son is surprised and astonished by new information he gathers at times. He is happy and tells jokes. He probably even tells jokes that some people think are stupid and not funny. He gets angry, throws stuff, and yells at people. And he weeps. He was and is like you and me in every way but was without sin.

At times it is easy to allow the death of Jesus to over shadow his life. In our minds we fast-forward the first 33 years of his life to get to the "good stuff." But the Father didn't just send Jesus into the world so he could slap a warm body on the cross.

The incarnation speaks to the astonishing reality that God was willing to become "one of us." Furthermore, the Son became the very best "one of us" who ever lived. The Son was the most fully human person who has ever been. Although he was (and is) God, he didn't cling to his rights as God. Instead, he chose to live a life like you and I in every way. At all points like us—yet without sin.

Irenaeus, a church father, says, "The glory of God is a man fully alive." Surely, God has never been more glorified than through the life of Jesus. No one has ever been more fully alive than Jesus. Yet, the death and resurrection of Jesus enable us to approach life as Jesus did. His death and resurrection make us alive for the first time. As we journey with Jesus, we are slowly becoming human.

RESTORATION

Perhaps you are quite skeptical about all of this. You're thinking, "Wow, it seems quite convenient for Jesus followers that he rose from the dead but . . . he's not here anymore . . . yeah. So Jesus is in heaven now and present with us here on earth? Sure . . . " For some, if Siri or TomTom can't give you directions to Jesus' physical location, it's not legitimate.

Michael Brooks who holds a PhD in quantum physics wrote a fascinating book called *13 Things that Don't Make Sense: The Most Baffling Scientific Mysteries of Our Time*. He writes: "The things that don't make sense, are in some ways, the only things that matter." Although Brooks doesn't seem to be a follower of Jesus, he encourages us not to sweep these mysteries that defy our understanding under the rug.

In his chapter "The Missing Universe," he explains:

Almost all of the universe is missing: 96 percent to put a number on it. The stars we see at the edges of distant galaxies seem to be moving under the guidance of invisible hands that hold the stars in place and stop them from flying off into empty space. According to our best calculations, the substance of those invisible guiding hands – known to scientists as dark matter – is nearly a quarter of the total amount of mass in the cosmos. Dark matter is just a name, though. We don't have a clue what it is.[12]

The universe is filled with vast amounts of mass and energy that we are unable to explain or understand. There is an entire world of reality that exists around us but that is beyond our ability to see it. Even in this room right now there are radio waves and light spectrums that my senses can't perceive. On a micro level there are bacteria, microbes, and atoms that I can't see.

We acknowledge all of that. So to say, "I can't see Jesus. I don't know where heaven is, so it must not be real" By that reasoning, we must reject the majority of what makes up the universe.

If we can trust what Scripture has to say about Jesus then we will understand some key truths: first, Jesus' glorified human body is enthroned in the place of supreme honor in heaven; second, Jesus' divine nature allows his spirit to be everywhere-present with us on earth; and third, the Church's union with Jesus makes us his spiritual body on earth.

Each of these ideas are loaded with meaning and mystery. They are worth considering because Jesus' continued activity today clues us in to what God is doing to restore the world. In this regard, there are two activities of Jesus that Scripture highlights in particular.

------

[12] Michael Brooks. *13 Things That Don't Make Sense: the Most Baffling Scientific Mysteries of Our Time*, Reprint ed. New York, NY: Vintage, 2009. 8.

1. Jesus is preparing a new city where we will live with him.

About 24 hours before his death in John 14, Jesus tells his disciples, "I am going away to prepare a place for you. And if I go I will come again so that where I am you may be also."

Although we cannot be with Jesus physically now, that's not the end of the story. The end of the story is when Jesus fully establishes his Kingdom on the earth. The New Jerusalem, a city about two-thirds the size of the continental US, descends from heaven. There we will dwell with God and his people forever. The face-to-face relationship with God that was lost in the Garden will be restored in the City.

2. Jesus is now exalted as the rightful Ruler of all things

"According to the working of his great might that he worked in Christ when he raised him from the dead and seated him at his right hand in the heavenly places, far above all rule and authority and power and dominion, and above every name that is named, not only in this age but also in the one to come. And he put all things under his feet and gave him as head over all things to the church, which is his body, the fullness of him who fills all in all." – Ephesians 1:19b-23

The resurrection stands as proof that God chose and anointed Jesus as King to rule the world. Yet the way we live in light of this reign creates tension. The people of God submit to the rule of Jesus. He is the head and we are his body. We desire for Jesus to rule in our lives although we are constantly seduced with the unworthy rule of competing affections.

Also, the world does not yet recognize God's reign—which creates even greater tension. Their refusal to recognize him as king does not change the fact that he is. If I pretend I am President of the United States—or even truly believe myself to be—all that pretending or believing doesn't mean much besides the fact that I am living a lie. The world doesn't submit to the rule of Jesus.

In 1 John 5, John says, "We know that the whole world lies under the sway of the evil one." Similarly in 2 Corinthians 4, Paul declares, "If the message of Jesus seems foolish it is foolish to those who are perishing. In their case the god of this age has blinded their eyes to keep them from seeing the light of the gospel. The glory of God in the face of Jesus Christ."

So the world is blind to the rule of Jesus. Our culture doesn't acknowledge King Jesus. Instead, the world lives in subjection to evil powers.

Jesus brought the rule of God near in his Kingdom. By moving into the neighborhood through the incarnation, he came to show us what a life under the authority of God looks like. Trusters-of-Jesus are now citizens of that Kingdom. Under Jesus' leadership, we can now participate with what God is doing in the world via the Kingdom.

Let's close our eyes for a moment and imagine standing with the disciples forty days after Jesus rose from the grave. With all our hearts, we desire for Jesus to clean house and establish his Kingdom right now. We want the pain to be over. We want corruption gone. We want the curse reversed. We want sin destroyed. We want to sit in triumph next to Jesus in the new kingdom. We want "what is" to be transformed into "what ought to be." And as this vision for the kingdom bubbles up inside of us, Jesus ascends. He leaves.

Jesus is saying something to us in that moment: "It's not time for you to share in my glory yet. It's not time for the consummation of the Kingdom. My Kingdom is now, but it is also not yet."

The vision that Jesus came to embody and impart to us could be expressed by the Hebrew word *shalom*. Shalom is closely tied to justice and righteousness. One could say that it is, in fact, the aim of justice and righteousness. Shalom is the way life ought to be. Tim Keller says, "It means complete reconciliation, a state of the fullest flourishing in every dimension—physical, emotional, social, and spiritual—because all relationships are right, perfect, and filled with joy."[13]

Only the God Jesus reveals makes such a life possible. This is the story of God's work to redeem humanity and restore all things. The question we must now engage is this: "How does this true story inform the stories we are living?"

Life Narrative #1: The Home Depot – "You can fix it, God can help."

The most popular application of the biblical story is that God's work through Jesus allows us to fix our lives with God's help. The story of Scripture is then distilled and edited in a way that supports this reading. This narrative is captured pristinely in the Christian-produced movie "Facing the Giants."

The film depicts a high school football coach who finds himself in "the badlands"—metaphorically speaking. The movie begins by showing how tough his life is. His football team stinks. The stove at home is broken. His car is old and unreliable. There is an unidentifiable hidden stench in his home. He and his wife are unable to get pregnant. He is on the chopping block due to his poor performance as the head football coach.

As the movie unfolds, Coach Grant melts down and calls out to God. As he begins to rely on God, everything changes. The football team begins to win. Someone gives him a brand new Ford pickup truck. His wife becomes pregnant. By the end of the movie, everything resolves itself.

We are prone to prefer stories where all the loose ends are tied up and everything flows in a predictably perfect sequence. That preference is reflected in the way we tell our own spiritual journey to others.

"Well I used to do this sin and that sin. And then I met Jesus and . . . well now I don't do that anymore." This is a booby-trapped good news.

---

[13] Timothy Keller. *Generous Justice: How God's Grace Makes Us Just.* New York, NY: Riverhead Books, 2012. 174.

My son James loves to engineer contraptions with his toys. Unfortunately the laws of physics make for a cruel playmate. Things break, snap off, or simply won't balance and fit together in the way he imagines. But there's good news in James' mind. He then optimistically verbalizes it: "Daddy will fix it."

Sometimes I can fix it. But there are other times where my inability to weld, mold plastic, and use a screwdriver (joking on that last one!) eliminates the possibility of "Daddy fixing it." But James has a backup plan in that scenario. "Grandpa will fix it!" Both his grandpas have a wider range of fix-it skills than I do. But sometimes grandpa can't fix it either.

If "Daddy will fix-it" is the life narrative we have distilled from the story of Jesus, we have misunderstood the story of Jesus and we have set ourselves up to live in extreme cognitive dissonance for our entire life. Here's how that life narrative fleshes itself out:

> How do you know if you're living in this "Home Depot Life Narrative?" Have you ever posted or read a social media update that read something like, "I got the job! God is good!" That scares me. That scares me because I think, "Wait a second. Is God good because you got the job? What if you hadn't got the job?"

We often think, "God is good . . . unless something bad is happening to me." The subtle belief that hides behind that will ruin people in a moment of crisis. Because what they are really saying is, "God is good when my life is good. When I am in the badlands, God is not good." Then when the conflict and confusion enter we moan and question the reality of God's goodness. We expect God to prove his goodness by giving us what we want. In *Glorious Ruin*, Tullian Tchividjian writes,

> God is not punishing you [for spilling your hot chocolate on the carpet, demonstrating lack of faith, deficient character, un-learned lessons, etc.]. He is not waiting for you to do something. You don't have to pull yourself up by your boot-

straps and find a way to conquer the odds, be stronger, or transform yourself into some better version of yourself.[14]

Later on he speaks to the exact storyline we are examining now,

> If the narrative we've adopted says that in order for our relationship with God to be legitimate, our life has to get better and our suffering get smaller, we set up an inescapable conflict, or what social scientists calls 'cognitive dissonance.' When our view of ourselves is at risk, honesty is always the first casualty. That is, when the gospel is twisted into a moral self-improvement scheme, self-deception is a foregone conclusion.

Living in this story requires lying to yourself and simplifying the way the world work's under God's rule. For a short while, this may appease your mind, but it will suffocate your heart. This narrative isn't functional. Let's look at another life narrative.

Life Narrative #2: "Some restoration now, complete restoration later."

What is the nature of God's restoring work in the world and in our lives? Is it higher income? Is it healing from sickness? Is it the answered prayer for a new car? Sometimes. Undeniably God cares about these fine details of our lives. However, God's renewing work is actually much bigger than these things. God's gracious provision is more than getting what we want. Through Jesus, he gives us what we need.

A while ago I sat on a plane discussing the future kingdom of Jesus with a college professor of Nordic Studies. He struggled to categorize his spirituality but threw out "deist" as a possibility. We discussed how Christians show up in the world. Why is

---

[14] Tchividjian, 55.

it that Christians are so often characterized by political anxiety and cultural fear?

During our conversation, I expressed the hope that Christians would have a restoring and healing influence in the world. "My hope is not in my ability to bring comprehensive healing." I shared, "My hope is in the fact that Jesus will do all of this when he sets up his Kingdom. I anticipate that. But to the degree that I can imagine what his kingdom will look like then, I should participate with the Spirit to help create that now."

Looking back, I suppose the Spirit was using me to paint a picture for Ben. A picture of Jesus as the Restorer of Culture. Of course, we aren't just called to discuss restoration—we are called to participate.

What does aligning ourselves with God's restoration look like? John Barry founded Jesus' Economy with a vision to create jobs and churches in places like Bihar, India. Now entrepreneurs and pastors are working together for the common good of Bihar.

Joe Baker launched Save the Storks as a new kind of pro-life movement. Now three out of five abortion-minded women who step into a Storks bus decide to keep their baby.

Unlike the naive Home Depot narrative, this second story allows us to sit in the very real tension that life confronts us with. Some restoration occurs now, but it is not comprehensive. When conflict and confusion enter your story you can hold to the truth, "I may not get answers about the 'why' of this problem, but I get Jesus. And he is better than answers." And in this second story, sometimes God restores things in and around us, and sometimes he doesn't. Why? Because the rule of Jesus has not yet been consummated in our world.

SUMMARIZING THE KINGDOM STORY

The Bible is one gigantic story of God's love for humanity and his desire for us to flourish through relationship with him.

Here's a plot synopsis of some of the key twists and turns in this story:

- The Trinity is the source of all love and life. Humans were created to enjoy friendship with God, to enjoy his creation, and to engage and explore the world creatively alongside God as mini-rulers.

- The first humans turned from God. Since then all humans have abandoned the source of love and life in exchange for false loves.

- As a result of this fall, humans are born separated and alienated from God. Our fundamental problem is that we love the wrong things. We long for life from that which cannot give life. Our desires are twisted. We are spiritually dead. And for the most part, we think everything is ok.

- Although humans don't seek God, God has sought reconciliation with us by sending Jesus, the God-man, to earth.

- Jesus shows us what trusting the Father and relying on the Holy Spirit are all about. He has demonstrated the nature of true life and true love. He has perfectly embodied the heart of God and what matters to God because he was and is God.

- Jesus was killed by people who claimed to know God because he said he was God. He died but then rose from the dead three days later. He hung around in his resurrected state for forty days before ascending into heaven and then sending another member of the Trinity (the Spirit whom he called "The Helper") to help his disciples live the life he had now made possible.

- Apprentices of Jesus are to trust in the work God has done through Jesus, repent, and be baptized. The essence of repentance is a change in one's object of worship. This means turning from sin (false loves) and turning to Jesus. Of course, it is not possible to change ourselves in such a way. We merely, trust God to do what he has promised. His helping grace enables our trust in his promises. We are now brought into the joy of God and all of life becomes about embracing grace. That grace is multifaceted and involves quite a few different elements.

KEY THEMES OF THE STORY

The Bible follows the trajectory of the hero-myth we looked at in Conversation 1. God himself is the hero. The way he offers his fullness to humanity is called "grace" in the Bible. Grace is fundamentally God's self-giving. In the story of God, when people respond to God's truth and his love, lives are transformed. When that takes place, there are certain results and themes that start to emerge in our lives.

- God credits us with a new, justified, status – We are credited with Jesus' righteousness by trust in his work on the cross. Jesus became our substitute on the cross; bearing the punishment we deserve and giving us the righteousness we could never obtain.
- God gifts us with a new heart – Before conversion our desires are evil and corrupt. Through regeneration the Holy Spirit gives us a new heart with new desires. This new core identity is "created after the likeness of Christ in true righteousness and holiness" (Ephesians 4:24). So not only are we credited righteousness through justification, we are imparted righteousness through the Spirit.
- God equips us for a new battle – Although our old nature is dead and no longer defines us, it left a wake of destruction behind. And although the sin that once defined us no longer does so, there remains a traitor within: the flesh. In fact, there is a trifecta of temptation that can distract us from treasuring Jesus. The corrupt world systems we live within, demonic forces, and the flesh all contribute to a full-scale spiritual war.
- God gifts us with a new family – This new family is the church. We are the "body of Christ." Jesus is our head, ruling from heaven. And we are his people, submitting to him as our head, carrying out his wishes. This new community becomes a huge part of our context for prac-

ticing the grace we have received from God. Together we share in Jesus' life and in Jesus' suffering.

- God equips us for a new mission – Jesus has commanded us to make disciples who make disciples. He has poured out the Holy Spirit to live within us, speak to us, encourage us, strengthen us, and lead us in this mission.

- God connects us with a new hope – Thanks to the work of Jesus, our hope rests solely on God's gift of himself to us. The gospel of Jesus is the only story that truly leads to life and love. How will that hope be realized? Jesus has bought up all the stock that exists for planet earth. Right now he's receiving "dividends." Christians are those dividends. But one day, Jesus will cash in all his stock and take full possession of the world that is rightfully his. God will bring heaven to earth and we will once again dwell with him, face-to-face.

THINK

- What elements of the story of God seem new or significant to you right now?
- How does the story of God confront the life narrative you live by?

LOVE

- What new values and desires does the story of God and his work stir in you?

DO

- Build a timeline that reflects your life narrative as it has been then draw a new timeline that reflects a new orientation towards the Kingdom.
- Share what you are discovering about yourself with a close friend or family member.

WHEN WE TRUST A BROKEN STORY
Conversation 3

Sometimes I do what I don't want to do. I hurt myself. I hurt others. You could truthfully say that I'm broken, but I'm not the only one. I have seen fellow followers of Jesus live a lot of brokenness. Whatever it means to align our lives with the story of God, it certainly doesn't result in the tidy "before" and "after" pictures you'd see on an infomercial.

Why do I allow my selfish ambitions to sabotage the possibility of truly loving others? Why did my Jesus-loving friend momentarily abandon hope and kill himself? How could a Christian leader I worked with cheat on his wife and wreck his ability to father his two young children?

The Bible teaches that every Christian is gifted a new heart and a new identity when we trust in Jesus. If so, why are there times when I don't want to follow Jesus? If the core of who I am is created after the likeness of Jesus in true righteousness and holiness then why do I still choose evil at times?

As fantastic as our new identity as disciples and kingdom citizens is, we cannot progress more than a couple inches in following Jesus before we realize that there is a very real civil war going on within us. Part of me desires Jesus. Other times I cheat on Jesus. What's going on?

Paul explains the inner struggle this way:

> For I do not understand my own actions. For I do not do what I want, but I do the very thing I hate. So now it is no

longer I who do it, but sin that dwells within me. For I know that nothing good dwells in me, that is, in my flesh. For I have the desire to do what is right, but not the ability to carry it out. For I do not do the good I want, but the evil I do not want is what I keep on doing. Now if I do what I do not want, it is no longer I who do it, but sin that dwells within me. – Romans 7:15, 17-20

THERE IS A WAR INSIDE EACH OF US

Paul wants to obey Jesus, but he doesn't sometimes. Sometimes his flesh—the sin that dwells in him—hijacks his will and causes him to do what he hates. How in the world can this be reconciled with all that Scripture teaches about our new identity?

Frequently folks have made the mistake of teaching that Christians have two natures, a new one and a sinful one. Or worse yet, "We are justified by Jesus but still rotten at the core." This misunderstanding occurs from viewing the "old man" or "old nature" as synonymous with "flesh." The two are not at all the same. So what does Paul mean by "flesh"?

In the Bible the English word translated "flesh" is two different Greek words that mean two different things in the original languages. At times flesh refers to our physical nature. There is nothing wrong or evil about our physical bodies. When the Greek word *sarx* is translated flesh, it has a different meaning. In Romans 7, Paul uses the Greek word *sarx* for flesh. Although that may sound tricky or technical, it's actually quite easy to determine how the word "flesh" is being used in the context of the passage. Clearly the "flesh" being spoken of here is referring to some sort of indwelling moral evil—not our physical bodies.

If a nation is invaded by a foreign nation and loses, a new government takes over. The surrendering country would be re-structured, re-ordered, and probably re-named to reflect the new rule. New flags would fly from flagpoles. Citizens adjust their allegiance to the new rule. Perhaps not everyone likes this new rule though. The movie *Red Dawn* depicts such a scenario in which a small band of citizens don't comply with the government takeover—instead fighting back with guerrilla warfare tactics.

If Jesus is your Lord, you have surrendered to his rule. Although you are now in the Kingdom of God you were born into the kingdom of darkness. You live in a world system that is under the sway of the evil one. So even though Jesus has raised a new flag within your heart, there are pockets of resistance within you. Like guerrilla fighters, they refuse to accept the rule of God. This is a picture of "the flesh" as Paul used in Romans 7.

Sometimes the faith we sell people is "Your life is going to be put back together and you are going to be a super amazing, creative person." Sorry. That's not the case. We continue to experience inner chaos. A battle rages between the rule of Jesus and our flesh. Will we walk in our new identity or allow the traitor within to have the last word?

Here's a truer picture of the faith: You can't fix yourself. Although you can expect some maturing and progressing over the course of your life the struggle never stops. The inner conflict is never eradicated. You don't become whole until heaven. So our hope is not in our ability to gradually repair ourselves. No. Our hope is that Jesus will one day perfect us when he brings heaven to earth.

Remember the four scenes of everyone's story we talked about earlier in the book? For the disciple of Jesus, Redemption is a past fact, a presently progressing reality, and a future promise. We have been rescued from the penalty and power of sin, are being rescued from the deceitfulness of sin, and will be rescued from the presence of sin.

For the disciple of Jesus, Restoration is something we only see flickers of. The story does not end on our deathbeds when people say, "Wow, they managed to fully overcome brokenness." Our stories find their ending and true beginning on the day Jesus completes the restoration he has promised—both in our souls and bodies and on earth.

TEMPTATION IS A STORY WAR

Shortcuts can backfire on you. Whether you think you know a shortcut on a road to get somewhere, or a shortcut to a friendship, or a shortcut to a project—we tend to try and find easier and more convenient ways to arrive at the same place. But shortcuts frequently backfire.

That's how temptation shows up in our lives. Temptation is like a shortcut to a good thing. In Matthew 4, Jesus experiences three temptations that highlight how many times the most powerful temptation is not to do something bad, but to do something good in the wrong way.

Specifically, Jesus is tempted to indulge a legitimate desire (eat), to believe something that is true (he is the Messiah), and to pursue a kingdom-minded shortcut (establish the Kingdom of God). These are all good things, which is exactly why these temptations were strategically chosen by Satan. Satan offers Jesus the chance to live a story with the same ending as God's perfect plan but with a different plot.

So what's the problem with these temptations? They don't seem so bad.

In the first temptation, Jesus was tempted to indulge a desire at the cost of a greater desire. There's a sad story in the Bible of a man who sold his birthright for a bowl of stew because he was hungry. This is the epitome of short-sightedness. It's easy to allow a legitimate desire to crowd out things that may be even more important.

In the second temptation, Jesus was tempted to believe a truth in isolation. That is, a truth isolated from the rest of the story of Scripture. It was only Jesus' knowledge of God's broader plans and purposes that allowed him to reject the sound byte truth that Satan fed him.

During the third temptation, Jesus was tempted to establish the Kingdom by temporarily worshipping the wrong thing. Satan was saying, "We can get to the last chapter of the story without any conflict. All you have to do is worship me."

As far as I can tell, every temptation I've ever faced has fit one of those three molds. Temptation comes to us in the form of a story. And that story will always tweak the details of the biblical story in some way. At that point, we are caught in the middle of two stories that war for our heart.

SIN IS TRUSTING A BROKEN STORY

The essence of sin is false love. When we love the wrong things in the wrong order, we've put our stock in a broken story. Rather than desiring God above all things, some misplaced desires flood our vision. If you have some perspective, it's probably not too difficult to look back and see how these broken stories have manifested in your life. You have pursued (and still pursue) loves that were "ultimate" for you but were also false.

Tristan's Story

From the moment Tristan first stepped into my car on the way to the coffee shop, he seemed burdened. We ordered drinks, sat down, and the whole situation came pouring out. He was confused about why he continued to look at pornography even though he didn't want to. Together, we began to unpack the broken story he was trusting in.

During our conversation, it became clear Tristan's deep longing was to be a husband and a father. The porn was a cheap substitute for the intimacy his soul craved. The porn promised to meet this desire, but it couldn't. His spirit was left sloshing around in a wake of sewage.

For Tristan, grasping the distinction between the true story of Jesus and the broken story of pornography was a turning point in his internal civil war. He was able to see that his good desire for intimacy was being hijacked and driven down a road that leads to death. So we talked about the road to life and truth. We spent the end of our time exploring the question, "How is God inviting you to you feed your desire for intimacy with him and with others?"

All of us are seduced by broken stories. For a moment, they promise hope, but if we follow them long enough they lead to frustration, pain, and an overwhelming emptiness. So how can we gain perspective in the midst of these story war?

The way we refuse false love is by catching a captivating picture of Jesus as the true and better lover of our souls. And our weapon for fighting the story wars is not willpower; it's worship. As we fixate on Jesus, we see that he is the real picture of human flourishing. Other stories of our good can't deliver. So worship (i.e., affection and desire for God) —not willpower—is what kills sin in our lives.

SIN CAMOUFLAGES GOD'S COMMITMENT TO YOUR JOY

A whole host of misconceptions and deceptions regarding the true nature of joy and pleasure have led to believers at times presenting themselves as instruments for sin rather than instruments of righteousness. For some reason, all of us have at times been roped into believing that sin has the corner on fun, pleasure, and joy. If we're honest, a life of obedience means a life of immense sacrifice—primarily sacrificing that which would be more fun and pleasurable. In reality, sin is counter-joy and counter-pleasure. When we come to understand this biblical truth it leads us one step closer to overcoming the deceitfulness of sin.

Listen to King David's heart in Psalm 16: "The lines have fallen to me in pleasant places; indeed, I have a beautiful inheritance. . . . You make known to me the path of life; in your presence there is fullness of joy; at your right hand are pleasures forevermore."

This is a far cry from the imagery of God that some of us have acquired. We may imagine him as a cosmic sheriff who cruises around writing citations for loud music at parties, riding a bike without a helmet, or ending speedy joy rides with blaring sirens and flashing lights. Instead, David describes God as the very source of joy and eternal pleasure. If God is the source of true joy and pleasure then whatever counterfeit temptations offer is clearly not the real thing.

Some of Jesus' final statements to the disciples express his desire for us to experience real joy. "As the Father has loved me, so I have loved you. Abide in my love. If you keep my commandments, you will abide in my love, just as I have kept my Father's commandments and abide in his love. These things I have spoken to you, that my joy may be in you, and that your joy may be full." The equation is clear. Conscious remembrance of Jesus' love for us leads to fruitful obedience of his commands, which in turn leads to experiencing the same level of joy he had—fullness of joy.

Obedience to God is not primarily an act of martyrdom although it often does involve self-sacrifice. Actually, the Bible says that Jesus' motivation for going to the cross in obedience was joy. Jesus "for the joy set before him endured the cross, despising the shame, and is seated at the right hand of the throne of God" (Heb. 12:2).

The benefit for Jesus going to the cross was the joy of bringing the people of God to himself for all eternity. The momentary cost was the shame of mockers, separation from the Father, and the physical pain. The analysis led to obedience for Jesus—as it always did. But hypothetically, if he hadn't obeyed the will of the Father, he wouldn't have endured the cross because of the cost of temporary shame and he would have been despising joy.

The connection is clear as we look at the example of Jesus. Choosing sin is despising joy. Sin offers joy but cannot deliver it. Satan offers cheap thrills as opposed to the eternal pleasure of God.

Scripturally it is clear that God is pro-obedience because he is pro-joy and pro-pleasure. Conversely, sin offers fleeting pleasures closely followed by feelings of dissatisfaction, guilt, and an increased appetite for more of the garbage we just ate. Sin is counter-joy and the sooner we grasp this the more readily we will choose the joy of abiding in the love of Jesus.

WE FACE A HOST OF INVISIBLE LIARS

In the Bible, demons are never mentioned without reference to God's authority over them. By making mention of Satan and demons in Scripture, God obviously wants us to know something. However, the central focus of Scripture is not gaining total knowledge into the spirit world but rather encountering the person and work of Jesus.

Similarly in Colossians 2, the focus of the text is not primarily on demons it is on Jesus. Namely, how Jesus disarmed demons at the cross and how our identity is now united with Jesus because of his triumph. Before discussing the purposes of demons and their opposition to followers of Jesus, let's ask a few basic questions.

Demons might be invisible to our eyes, but their effects are very real. There is more that composes reality than what our senses can perceive. For example, there are different types of light waves on the electromagnetic spectrum—microwaves, x-rays, radio waves, gamma rays, ultraviolet, infrared, as well as visible. In fact, there is all sorts of electromagnetic action around you right now, but you can only perceive some of it—the visible light. The same is true in the spiritual realm and with spiritual beings.

According to Scripture, Satan and demons were created as angels to serve God, but Satan (who was called Lucifer at that point), wanted to set himself up as God so he rebelled and one-third of the angels decided to go with him. So demons are evil spiritual beings who oppose the things of God. Why? Satan can't stomach a story centered on God. Ever since his fall his forces have been whispering broken stories to humanity.

How should we respond to the reality of these invisible liars? If you think about them too much that will create a tendency towards fear. They aren't the centerpiece in the story of God but they are mentioned in Scripture. If I was a rotten guy and wanted to slash your tires, my best case scenario is for you to be oblivious of the impending threat.

Basically everything that Satan and demons do fits into one of three evil categories. These are the ways that demons would like to be involved in your life: Deceive, accuse, and tempt.15 We see two of these in Colossians 2. In this passage, demons are trying to deceive and trying to accuse. They also seek to encourage and energize sin.

Paul begins the passage in Colossians 2 by warning the church not to be deceived by beliefs that originate from demons. And in the second portion of the passage Paul talks about how the legal grounds the demons had to accuse us with because of our sin—that ground is destroyed (v13-15). Paul's central point in this text is that faith in Jesus' forgiveness disables demons.

If you actually believe the good news that your sin was paid for at the cross and the legal demands against you were cancelled—that is absolutely crippling to the forces of darkness who oppose you. Faith in Jesus' forgiveness disables demons because it removes their grounds for accusation.

Demons also aim to deceive. So Paul encourages us to not be taken captive by faulty human traditions. Apparently these errant paradigms come from "the elemental spirits."

If we were going to biblically define "elemental spirits" we could say they are the evil supernatural powers that control the basic principles of the world system. In other words, we are talking about demons that use their energy to influence culture, governments, worldviews, philosophies, and obviously in this context Christians. 1 John 5 tells us: "We know that the whole world lies under the sway of the evil one." So according to Scripture, many of the prevailing trends and basic principles of culture are the result of undercover work by elemental spirits—demons.

Based off this concept it makes sense that demons are deeply, deeply involved in influencing religion. Deceptions like Islam, Buddhism, Mormonism, Jehovah Witness, Scientology, and so much more—are demonic projects that are incredible accomplishments for the powers of darkness. Any religion that excludes the full message of who Jesus is and why he came might have bits of truth, but they are lies and deceptions that according to Scripture originate from demons. The gods that these religions worship are real and these religions are full of real power and spiritual experiences because these gods are demons who reward their followers.

A few years ago, my wife and I took our son to a rinky-dink circus in Minnesota. They were juggling fire, shamelessly trying to sell cheap toys, selling you six peanuts for a buck because they were "special circus peanuts." And they had plenty of trained animals too. Lions, and tigers, and camels, oh my! But the biggest was the elephant. And it was amazing to watch these animals get bossed around by a petite lady. Watching it made me think, "How much power does a tiny trainer have over a giant elephant?" The answer is, "However much power the elephant allows her to have!" Does that elephant have to submit? Absolutely not. But it can yield control and influence to the circus woman.

How much power does a demon have over you? The answer is the same. Demons can only influence disciples to the degree we choose to listen. So don't listen. Don't be deceived. Don't submit. Demons have no right to invade or influence a disciple of Jesus because Jesus has set us free from the penalty of sin and the kingdom of darkness. We now live in the Kingdom of Light.

WHAT IF I CHEAT ON JESUS?

The aftermath of sin is a dust cloud of complex feelings. Part of moving towards health means asking ourselves the question, "What is going on in my soul right now? What specifically am I feeling right now and why?"

When I speak harshly to my son, I've stirred up pain for myself and for him. For a moment, I trusted the broken story that the best way to father my son is to control him. And because that story wasn't working I got frustrated. I had to find another way to control him and that meant yelling. In doing so I was loving a self-constructed ideal of my son rather than actually loving the boy right in front of me. In pursuit of that vision, I lost my temper.

It's ok to feel the weight of that. But as I sit there, sometimes weeping, breathing in the pollution I've stirred up, there are other voices that vie for my ear. What do those voices have to say? The enemy may heap guilt and condemnation upon me.

- My flesh may lead me to mentally assent to the sin but then offer a quick and empty confession to God.

- My flesh might lead me to think that God's grace certainly cannot be laid hold of too easily . . . no, before going to God I must mourn properly and possibly even clean myself up a bit through a probationary period of restitution. Afterwards the benefits of relationship with God can be resumed.
- I may try to pay a penalty for my sin by praying a super-eloquent prayer. My eloquence is what will make me right with God, not grace.
- I may try to sweep everything under the rug by ignoring the Holy Spirit's invitation to confess. This damages and hardens my conscience. I am effectively "turning down the volume" on the speakers that allow me to hear God's voice. This makes it more difficult for me to hear him in the future—because I have chosen not to.

There are a lot of ways to harm ourselves and others by responding poorly in the aftermath of trusting a broken story.

First, acknowledge the broken story you have trusted by exposing and identifying it. Identify the motive behind your misplaced love.

All sin is at it's core disbelief in God and his gospel. We must understand the way in which we have disbelieved God which led us into the particular action of sin. The external action or deed is a manifestation of what's going on in the heart. Therefore, we must not settle for modifying our behavior, but rather asking, "What am I not believing about God and his gospel?" On this point, John Piper insightfully states: "Sin is what you do when you heart is not satisfied with God . . . which means that the power of sin's promise is broken by the power of God's."[15]

Our flesh often leads us to fight sin with sin. We are motivated to eliminate a vice by another vice. For example, we don't reject gossip per se, only gossip that would make us look bad to others. Personally I find that I am often more concerned with appearing humble than actually being humble. This is pride. In

---

[15] Brian Hedges. *Christ Formed in You: The Power of the Gospel for Personal Change.* Wapwallopen, PA: Shepherd Press, 2010. 181.

scenarios like this, we inject ourselves with a virus in order to cure a troubling symptom.

This is not the way of Jesus. Such thinking fits well if our goal is only behavior modification. However, Jesus is more concerned with our hearts and motives than with our behavior and actions. This is so because "it is possible to change what we do, even reducing the frequency of certain sins, without actually becoming more pure in heart."

Second, be honest about the pain your sin has brought to yourself and others.

"It's no big deal." This phrase is often given in response to apologies. But sin is a big deal. Sin adds to the brokenness of the world. Sin brings pain into the world and that pain must land somewhere. That's what the cross was about. When the Father sent Jesus to earth he wasn't thinking, "Sin is no big deal."

We must assess the real damage done in our lives, to our relationship with God, to others around us, and the potential harm to our future because of particular sin. Part of fully processing our sin is feeling the weight of its danger and potential destructiveness (Matthew 7:13). It is not enough to know that petting a crocodile is against the zoo's rules if we do not also agree that it is dangerous and potentially deadly.

Finally, we must grieve our sin while celebrating God's grace. This is the heart attitude of repentance. Repentance is nothing less than changing what we are worshipping. Turning from the broken story we trusted and placing all our stock in the story of God.

It's important to understand that repentance does not put us back in God's good graces. Repentance acknowledges that despite our faithlessness, we are still in God's good graces. Repentance does not earn us grace. It simply consciously brings to remembrance the grace that we have already received.Jesus is the Better Water

WE THIRST FOR

A woman, a Samaritan, came to draw water. Jesus said, "Would you give me a drink of water?" (his disciples had gone to the village to buy food for lunch.) The Samaritan woman taken back, asked, "How come you, a Jew, are asking me, a Samaritan woman, for a drink?" (Jews in those days wouldn't be caught dead talking to Samaritans.)

Jesus answered, "If you knew the generosity of God and who I am, you would be asking me for a drink, and I would give you fresh, living water."

The woman said, "Sir, you don't even have a bucket to draw with, and this well is deep. So how are you going to get this 'living water'? Are you a better man than our ancestor Jacob, who dug this well and drank from it, he and his sons and livestock, and passed it down to us?"

Jesus said, "Everyone who drinks this water will get thirsty again and again. Anyone who drinks the water I give will never thirst—not ever. The water I give will be an artesian spring within, gushing fountains of endless life."

The woman said, "Sir, give me this water so I won't ever get thirsty, won't ever have to come back to this well again!"

Jesus then launches into a mini-teaching about true worship and even a prophetic word about where worship will take place. The woman responds by saying:

"I don't know about that. I do know that the Messiah is coming. When he arrives, we'll get the whole story."

"I am he," said Jesus. "You don't have to wait any longer or look any further."

Jesus is the water you and I are really looking for. With him we have the whole story. Yet so often my prayers are asking God to give me another cup, another story. Rather than drinking of the true story of Jesus I ask God to help my false loves work better. I ask God to purify the toilet water I'm drinking so that it satisfies me. But in the midst of our collective brokenness, Jesus assures us, "I am the Rescuer you have been looking for. I am the Lover you have been looking for. You don't have to wait any longer or look any farther."

THINK

- What false loves and broken stories are most seductive to you right now? How is the gospel a true and better story?

LOVE

- How would your life look different if you were treasuring Jesus supremely?
- What does repenting and re-orienting around Jesus need to look like for you?

DO

- What trusted person can you share your struggle with?
- Who might you need to express repentance and/or confession to?

THE FATHER, SON, AND HOLY SPIRIT
Conversation 4

"You can do that with a team of voices?" I remember thinking that when I discovered really good acapella. I was wowed by groups like The Coats at the Washington State Fair and the skillful covers of Pentatonix.

A band or choir will typically follow along with the melody of a tune, hitting notes in unison together. But I'm sure you've also heard of harmony. This is how acapella groups make their living. When harmonizing, different voices sing different pitches, creating rich, textured layers that sound ever-so-sweet to our ears.

Bruce Ware explains how harmony exemplifies God's relationship with himself:

> The three members of the Godhead work together in harmony. Not in unison, but in harmony. Unison expresses a form of unity yet it has no texture or richness. Harmony however communicates the idea of unified expression but only through differing yet complementary parts. You have different voices in different pitches.[16]

The doctrine of the Trinity acknowledges that God is one unified essence and three harmonious, distinct but co-equal

---

[16] Bruce Ware. *Father, Son, & Holy Spirit: Relationships, Roles, and Relevance*. Wheaton, IL: Crossway, 2005. 42.

persons: God the Father, God the Son, and God the Holy Spirit. Each member of the Trinity functions in a unique role but always in cohesion and unity with the other members. Consider this conversation an introduction to each person of the Trinity.

THE TRINITY IS ESSENTIAL IN THE STORY OF GOD

What makes understanding the three-in-one harmony of God essential? Quite simply, each member of the Trinity makes salvation possible. Therefore, if the Trinity is not true then our understanding of salvation is incorrect and must be modified.

Even in the Old Testament, we are introduced to a three-in-one understanding of God. "Hear O' Israel, the Lord our God is one." The Hebrew word used for "one" here is *ehad*. The same word is also used in Genesis 2:24 to speak of Adam and Eve becoming one. It connotes the clear understanding of not only being one in uniqueness but also speaks of a unity that is actually a union of several persons.

The redeeming work of the Trinity is highlighted further by a plethora of key New Testament passages. Perhaps most notably is the Great Commission, where Jesus commands his disciples to go make disciples. How often do we connect the command to make disciples with the Trinity? Yet the text says we are to "baptize into the name of the Father, Son, and Holy Spirit."

Therefore, becoming a follower of Jesus means we are acquainted with the three-in-one God and we are invited to share in the intimacies and joy of the Trinity. Jesus vividly describes this through a prayer to the Father we overhear in John 17. The invitation to Christianity is an invitation to receive life from the Trinity and enjoy the fullness of the Trinity. Our hearts are warmly drawn in as we become familiar with the unique roles of each member, and how each harmonious voice works together to provide and perfect our salvation.

WHAT MAKES THE FATHER A FATHER?

God the Father is not the Father because he created the world. All of humanity is not one family with God as our Father. That is not the language of Scripture. God is the Father because within the Trinity he is the Father of the Son. The Son never came into being or was born. Instead the Father and the Son have always existed together in perfect love, sharing the same essence.

The Father delights in the Son. He pours his life and his love into the Son. The Son responds to the Father's love by enjoying him and reveling in the relationship they share.

When we place our trust in the work of Jesus to cover our sins and to give us new life, we are united with Jesus. Our identity and our destiny is now linked with him forever. And so the Father of the Eternal Son actually becomes our Father.

Because Jesus is the Son, now we (who trust in him) are sons and daughters. Because Jesus is the heir of all things, now we are joint-heirs.

The Father Longs to Father Us

It is one thing to have God as our Father. It is another thing to let him father us.

I didn't pray to God as Father until a few years ago. It took actual practice and was quite difficult for me to begin to think of God as my dad. It wasn't because I had a bad dad or a neglectful dad or an absent dad. But my heart was not open to allowing God to father me. I was ok with having a Savior but not a Dad. I was ok with Jesus saving me from my junk, but I didn't want the embrace with the Father that came afterward. I'm finally discovering the beauty of being carried by Jesus into the arms of the Father. And this embrace, this belonging, is unconditional.

When it comes down to it, don't we really want to belong? No matter what our age, we crave belonging. Many of us want that specifically from a father. We long for a father.

Imagine a Father who takes you out of the poverty of your sin and makes you a member of his family.

Imagine belonging to a Father who puts his arms around you after you mess up and says, "Let me hold you. I love you. I will always, always love you."

Imagine knowing that you are fully accepted by this wonderful Father. That he will never walk out on you. If you walk out, he will lovingly pursue you. He won't give up on you because he is relentlessly committed to you.

Jesus introduces us to such a Father—his Father. He claims you as a sons and daughters. He says that you belong. The question we face then becomes, "Will you let him father you?"

Donald Miller expresses his personal grappling with these own questions in his book *Father Fiction*. He recounts a specific conversation with "John"—the man who came closest to filling the role of father in his life.

By the time we got back to the house, Terri and the kids were asleep. John and I sat in the den and watched Sports Center for a while. During commercials, he would mute the television and make small talk about some of the trips he had coming up, wondering out loud how he was going to get around once arriving in New Zealand, wondering how many days he should spend there as opposed to Australia. He was saying all this with some regret, and you could tell he didn't like being away from his family. But during the last commercial break, he started talking again about being a father, and I could tell he was doing it more for me than just to reminisce. He told me that when Terri gave birth to Chris and he held his son in his arms for the first time, it was the closest he had ever been to understanding to love of God. He said that though he had never met this little person, this tiny baby, he felt incredible love for him, as though he would lie down in front of a train if he had to, that he would give up his life without so much as thinking about it, just because this child existed. John set this love beside other relationships, but they didn't compare. In other relationships, the person he knew had to earn his love. Even with his own father, John learned to love him, and with his wife they had fallen in love over several years, becoming closer and closer friends. But it wasn't that way with his children. His love for them was instantaneous, from the moment of their birth. They had performed nothing to earn his love other than be born. It was the truest, most unconditional love he had known. John said if his love for Chris was the tiniest inkling of how God loved us then he had all the security in the world in dealing with God, because he knew, firsthand, what God's love toward him felt like, that it was complete. "I'm just saying, Don, if God is our Father, we've got it good. We've got it really good."[17]

God the Father is a perfect Father with a loyal love, complete understanding, and a trustworthy heart. Part of experiencing a relationship with God means allowing ourselves to fall into the arms of God the Father.

The Father Secures Us

Much of our lives are spent attempting to secure our own private and public world. It doesn't take much life experience to realize that none of us are very good at controlling our world. And when you can't control your world it often seems the only alternative is to live in anxiety, fear, and stress. The worst part is there doesn't seem to be another approach to life. Inevitably others let us down by failing to provide, to nurture, and to accept us unconditionally. So although we do not care and provide for ourselves perfectly, we believe there will be no one else to do the job if we step back. Although this seems to be the way things are, it does not describe reality. It does not describe the way the world actually is.

The teaching of Jesus describes an invisible heavenly Father whose compassionate essence is depicted through the life of Jesus himself. Jesus explains to us that our kingdom is too small and our king is too finite.

---

[17] Donald Miller. *Father Fiction: Chapters for a Fatherless Generation.* NY: Howard Books, 2011. 49-50.

In Matthew 6, Jesus highlights how our anxiety about the details of life is rooted in our delusional attempt at controlling life. He then contrasts that anxiety with the carefree nature of the birds and flowers who are always provided for by the invisible creator God. Jesus tells us, "Your heavenly Father knows your needs."

How might you move through life differently if you truly believed that every part of your existence lay in hands of a good and caring Father? A Father who not only knows your needs but is capable of meeting them with his limitless power. A Father who knows your needs and who will withhold no good from you because he is good. A Father who knows you completely and also loves you completely.

Jesus explains to us that *this is reality*. The concept that we rule our own universe is actually a misconception. And our acute awareness of our finiteness can do nothing but stack worry upon worry in our lives. Jesus asks us to relinquish the illusion of control and exchange it for trust in the goodness of our Father. He challenges us in this way:

> But seek first the kingdom of God and his righteousness, and all these things [security, freedom, validation, belonging] will be added to you. There is a ruler wiser and more powerful than you. The Creator God, the King of the universe, your heavenly Father invites you to walk away from your imaginary throne and to bow before his. He invites you to participate in his Kingdom by living with an awareness of his rule and allowing his kingship to re-order your world.

The Son Manifests the Life of God

Have you ever wondered what God is like? The answer to that question is Jesus. Jesus is the exact representation of God's nature (Heb. 1:3). Jesus perfectly reflects the character of God. The Father sent the Son into the world to display his heart for the world and his purposes for the world.

The theme of Jesus' life and teaching was the kingdom of God. He proclaimed the rule of God by saying, "The kingdom of

God is here. The kingdom of God is among you." What becomes very clear when reading the story of Jesus' life in Scripture is that his presence was synonymous with the presence of the kingdom of God. His life perfectly testified to the rule of God. For example, Jesus says:

> Truly, truly I say to you the Son can do nothing of his own accord, but only when he sees the Father doing. For whatever the Father does, that the Son does likewise. For the Father loves the Son and shows him all that he himself is doing. . . . For as the Father has life in himself, so he has granted the Son also to have life in himself. – John 5:19-20, 26

Elsewhere Jesus explains:

> When you have lifted up the Son of Man, then you will know that I am he, and that I do nothing on my own authority, but speak just as the Father taught me. And he who sent me is with me. He has not left me alone, for I always do the things that are pleasing to him. – John 8:28

It seems the whole of Jesus ministry was a response to what he heard when he was watching and listening. As he observed the will of the Father through the illumination of the Scriptures by the Spirit, or heard the voice of the Spirit during a moment of need—Jesus then acted accordingly. Jesus did only what he heard the Father speak to him.

In this way, Jesus shows us how to embrace the limitations of our humanity by living in trust in the Father and dependence on the Spirit. Of course, Jesus does far more than simply reveal God and the Kingdom of God. He actually brings us back to God. We will discuss this in the next conversation.

The Spirit Helps Us

When my oldest son James was three, we had a conversation about being bossy. It went something like this:

Me: "That sounded pretty bossy James. Bossy means that you tell other people what to do and try to make them do what you want."

James: "Oh ok. I'm really sorry daddy. I will never be bossy again."

Me: "Well that's a nice thing to say James. But you probably will be bossy again sometime though. That's because we aren't strong enough to change ourselves. How about you ask Jesus for some 'love energy' to try and change your heart? We need his help and he really wants to help us."

Since that conversation I've been so proud of James. He will still say bossy things occasionally, but he has a new self-awareness. He immediately tilts his head and asks me sheepishly, "Ummm, dad, was that a little bit bossy?"

In that conversation, I didn't fully unpack the intricacies of God's triune nature. I'm not always sure how to explain things that I don't grasp myself, but it's a real joy to have those practical moments of learning with him.

At some point, I'll need to more fully explain the way that Jesus gives us energy to love God and love other people (what we call "love energy" in our household discussions). The way that Jesus helps us is by giving us the same Spirit that energized his human life.

The Holy Spirit empowered Jesus' ministry and raised Jesus from the dead. In the lives of individual believers, the Spirit takes up residence within every believer at their moment of initial faith. He incorporates us into the Body of Christ. He seals each believer and reminds us that we belong to God. He teaches, guides, helps, encourages, energizes, and comforts Christians.

The Holy Spirit is such a dynamic, personal gift to us that Jesus actually said before his death, "It is to your advantage that I go away because after I leave the Helper will come." If we take these words at face value, it means the Spirit showcases the supremacy of Jesus, draws us into the abundant life of Jesus, and continues the work of Jesus in a way that was not possible prior to the ascension.

The Spirit Draws Us to Jesus

The Holy Spirit serves God's redemptive purposes by pointing people to Jesus. The Holy Spirit is the lead missionary on planet earth today.

Imagine God the Father sitting on a plush leather chair, waiting for you to stop by. Jesus says that he is the door into that space with the Father. No one can come to the Father except through him.

If Jesus is the door, the Holy Spirit is the neon sign in the alley pointing you towards the door. No one finds the door without following the direction that the Holy Spirit gives. The Spirit draws us to Jesus. The Spirit causes us to pause and to consider the significance of the person of Jesus for our lives and our world.

Sometimes folks get hung up on the issue of those who haven't heard. "But this remote indigenous tribe has never heard of Jesus! How can God hold everyone on earth accountable to a story that not everyone has heard?"

The drawing work of the Holy Spirit is an important part of the answer to this question. This remote indigenous tribe may not have found the door but they do have the neon sign. If they follow the directions the sign offers, they will find the door. That's what the Spirit does. The Holy Spirit is the person who testifies of Jesus, points to Jesus, softens hearts to Jesus, reveals the deity of Jesus, exposes our sinfulness and our need for Jesus. And Jesus tells us the Holy Spirit will do that for everyone. Even if they have never heard the name of Jesus (see Jn. 16:8-11).

How specifically does the Spirit point us to Jesus? He uses the inner witness of conscience (Rom. 2:14-16) and the external witness of creation (Ps. 19). He may also orchestrate relationships and events in our lives in a way that stirs up new thoughts and understanding about who God is. All of the Spirit's work is to bring us to trust in Jesus and what God has done for us through Jesus (Jn. 15:26).

The Spirit Motivates and Animates our Lives

In Luke 11, Jesus is teaching the disciples how to pray and he begins to talk about asking God for good gifts. He promises that God wants to give good gifts when we ask. He then instructs us that the best gift we can ask for is the Holy Spirit (v. 13). That's high praise for the Holy Spirit!

The Holy Spirit comes highly recommended from Jesus. Jesus could honestly tell us that the Holy Spirit is the best gift the Father gives because Jesus himself enjoyed an intimate relationship with the Holy Spirit. How do we know? We know based on the same criteria we'd use to evaluate any relationship between two people. "What good things flow from that relationship? What fruit is produced from this friendship?"

In the case of Jesus and the Spirit, Galatians 5 summarizes the product of their relationship: love, joy, peace, patience, kindness, faithfulness, gentleness, and self-control. We run into a problem when we try to bear the same fruit as Jesus without pursuing the same Spirit that empowered him. Jesus never intended for us to imitate him without the help of the Helper.

The Message translation describes the fruit of friendship with the Holy Spirit in this way,

> He brings gifts into our lives, much the same way that fruit appears in an orchard—things like affection for others, exuberance about life, serenity. We develop a willingness to stick with things, a sense of compassion in the heart, and a conviction that a basic holiness permeates things and people. We find ourselves involved in loyal commitments, not needing to force our way in life, able to marshall and direct our energies wisely. – Galatians 5:22-23

This is what it means to "live freely, animated and motivated by God's Spirit."

INVITED INTO THE JOYFUL LIFE OF THE TRINITY

Through Jesus, we have been invited to participate in the joyful life of the Trinity. The Christian experience should be constantly receiving more of God the Father, God the Son, and God the Helper. This is the best story we could imagine.

THINK

- What seems new or different about this understanding of God?
- Which person of the Trinity seems most foreign in your experience? Which is easiest to relate to?

LOVE

- Have a conversation with the Father asking him to widen your vision and stir your affection for each person of the Trinity so you can experience a deeper love for him.

DO

- Read John 17. Record your insights and observations as it relates to our conversation. Translate these reflections into a conversation with God.
- Spend some time reflecting, journaling, or blogging about the significance of the Trinity or how you hope to grow in relating to God the Father, the Son, and the Spirit.

HOW GRACE RE-WRITES OUR STORIES
Conversation 5

Let's imagine ourselves as Jesus' neighbors in the first-century. As Jews, we are oppressed by the Roman empire. Because our nation isn't a threat to Rome, we've been allowed a few national leaders—such as Herod. But guys like Herod are so unstable I'm not sure which is worse—our national leadership or the Roman Empire.

As children, we grew up hearing the mighty acts of Yahweh and how he delivered our people from violent oppressors over and over again. Yahweh brought us out of Pharaoh's cruel grip in Egypt through many wonders. Yahweh used judges to deliver us from pagan tribes and nations around us. After seventy years in exile, God brought us back to our homeland from Babylon. For our entire history as a people, God's favor has been synonymous with physical deliverance from our enemies. So where is God's favor now? Where is God now?

Then, out of the tiny town of Nazareth, Jesus emerges preaching, "The Kingdom of God is here." He quotes the words of the prophet Isaiah, "I'm here to preach good news to the poor, to proclaim release from darkness for the prisoners, and freedom for the captives. This is the year of the Lord's favor."

Everyone brims with excitement for this imminent triumph. Almost every day those closest to Jesus are asking him: "Will you set up the kingdom today?" "How about tomorrow?" "When, Jesus, when?" (Mk. 10:35-45).

A week before the Passover celebration, Jesus and his disciples arrive in Jerusalem. They are mobbed by wild enthusiasts. A spontaneous parade erupts. Thousands line the streets. Everyone is screaming, "Blessed is the King who comes in the name of the Lord!" and "Hosanna!" (Which means "Save, now!") "Didn't the prophets say that our king would come to us humble and riding on a donkey?" (Jn. 12:12-19).

Within days, the religious leaders place Jesus on trial before Pontius Pilate, a local Roman ruler. They accuse him, "This man says he is the promised Messiah King!" Pilate turns to Jesus and asks, "Are you the King of the Jews?" Jesus answers, "You have said so" (Jn. 18:19-24).

Those words were his death sentence. As Jesus suffered on the cross, the accusations were spelled out above his head, "This is Jesus, the King of the Jews." Then the religious leaders flip out again saying to Pilate, "Change it to say, 'This man said he was the king of the Jews.'" But Pilate said, "What I have written, I have written" (Jn. 19:28-40).

That day, the King of the Jews died. And with him, the hope of a nation or so it seemed.

Three days later the man who said he was King of the Jews rose from death! In the weeks that follow, he appeared to hundreds of his followers, eating, drinking, and conversing with them.

Now the question would seem to be a no-brainer, but with Jesus one can never be too sure . . . it's always better to ask. Jesus has now been alive again for forty days, teaching about the kingdom of God. He has gathered the disciples closest to him in Jerusalem and told them not to leave. Surely, the delay is that carpenter Jesus is manufacturing the office furniture that will furnish the new government. It can't be much longer . . .

So the disciples ask, "Lord, will you at this time restore the kingdom to Israel?" Jesus then says:

He said to them, "It is not for you to know times or seasons that the Father has fixed by his own authority. But you will receive power when the Holy Spirit has come upon you, and you will be my witnesses in Jerusalem and in all Judea and Samaria, and to the end of the earth." And when he had said these things, as they were looking on, he was lifted up, and a cloud took him out of their sight. And while they were gazing into heaven as he went, behold, two men stood by them in white robes, and said, "Men of Galilee, why do you stand looking into heaven? This Jesus, who was taken up from you into heaven, will come in the same way as you saw him go into heaven" – Acts 1:7-11

At this point, the disciples are overwhelmed and confused. What was supposed to be the moment of triumph has turned into Jesus disappearing. This day is not turning out like the disciples had hoped.

As Jesus ascends, his leaving creates tension. But Jesus promised that even in this "in-between" age of human history, he would always be with us. Jesus gives us the gift of himself as we seek to follow him now.

HOW IS JESUS "WITH US"?

When someone dies, people often say things like, "Uncle Jerry will always be with us . . . in our hearts." Or, "Her memory will live on as we treasure her in our hearts." Or maybe, "I know that Sharon is looking down on us right now and she is smiling with joy."

Is this what we mean when we say that Jesus is "with us"? After all, we can't see him. How can you fully experience the presence of a person who you can't see? In order to start understanding the answer to these questions, we have to realize that the curtain hasn't closed on Jesus' interaction with the world. Jesus relocated, but in a deeper sense he didn't really leave.

The perfect obedience and humility of Jesus is now being honored by the Father. For this reason, Jesus' ascension not only involved a physical relocation (earth to heaven) but it also involved a change of position and authority.

The ascension pictures how the Father is now giving Jesus the throne. On earth, Jesus was directing glory towards the Father, but now the Father is directing glory towards the Son. The way that the Father now exalts Jesus is reflected in the special seat of honor Jesus is given in heaven. He now sits at the right hand of the Father (see Pss. 48:10, 80:15-16, 89:13).

Although Jesus' physical body is seated in heaven, his divine nature allows his spirit to be everywhere-present with us on earth. Furthermore, Jesus has poured out to us the same Holy Spirit that energized his life. And Jesus is actively working in our world. Wherever the Holy Spirit is working Jesus' Spirit is also at work. The two are distinct but united. Together but not the same (see Acts 16:7, Phil. 1:19).

Before the cross, Jesus says, "It is to your advantage that I go away because when I go I will send the Helper" (Jn. 16:7). In Acts 1, Jesus promises again that he will send the Holy Spirit to empower us for the life and the mission he has given us. Jesus also promises he will never leave us or forsake us.

So Jesus is present with us spiritually, and he has also poured out the Holy Spirit who will help us walk in the footsteps of Jesus and love Jesus.

But the Holy Spirit is not the only way that Jesus remains with us today. The Church's union with Jesus makes us his spiritual body on earth.

Bodies and heads have to be connected. If not . . . well things can get a little ugly. Jesus is the spiritual head of the church and the church is the spiritual body of Jesus on the earth. Our job is to listen to the brains of the operation so that collectively, the church reflects the will of the head.

This image is a picture of what it means to be "in Christ" or to be "united with Christ." That means that our identity is now linked with him. His death on the cross means the death of our old identity rooted in sin and death. His resurrection means that our souls are made alive to God and that we no longer need to fear death because life with God is now our future hope. One day we will be glorified and have resurrected bodies as Jesus does.

The Bible is clear that Jesus is still "with us" (Mat. 28:20). But what is the personal meaning of his presence with us? What are the implications of being united to him? In a word: "Grace."

Grace is a word worthy of fleshing out. We cannot assume the definition of a word of such substance.

STORYING OURSELVES INTO GRACE

In 1988, river blindness was ravaging West Africa. Nearly 20 million people were affected worldwide and hundreds of thousands were completely blind. In many villages, people believed that one automatically grows blind as they age. Of course, many did not live to be "old" since the disease cut life expectancy by decades.

The disease spreads by tiny blackflies that breed near streams. The flies pick up the larvae of a parasite called *Onchocerca* when they bite infected people. Later when they bite someone, the parasite spreads. The baby parasites spread throughout the host's body lengthening to as much as two feet and living for as long as fourteen years. They procreate too and can produce as many as 200 million microworms in a human body. These worms spread and cause severe itching. When they reach the eye the result is blindness.

All potential solutions had reached a dead end. Pesticides were not able to fully destroy the flies. The few drug treatments that did work could not be massively applied and required medical supervision.

As devastation unfolded in Africa, pharmaceutical giant, Merck, was testing a new drug on cows they called ivermectin. The drug fights ear mites in cats and heart-worms in dogs. One researcher noticed that the drug was effective against an obscure horse parasite called *Onchocerca cervicalis*—a close cousin to the parasite associated with river blindness.

Merck was faced with a challenge. Should they spend millions of dollars developing a drug that was only needed by those who couldn't afford it? They did. Mectizan was the result. The following years they spent hundreds of millions of dollars of their stockholders money and their personal profit and resources to research, develop, and distribute the drug to those who needed it but could never afford it. Their leadership committed that they would give Mectizan away for free *forever* to those who needed it. As a result, river blindness has been eradicated.[18]

This story of incredible generosity is a microcosm of God's grace to us. We need help in making sense of grace because the grace of God is so counter-intuitive and outlandish that we must be storied into it somehow. The true story of river blindness allows us to see facets of Gods' grace that might difficult to see otherwise.

First, grace is help we receive when we are unable to help ourselves. Second, the nature of grace is self-giving. Third, the vision of grace is health, well-being, and human flourishing. Of course, the truest story of grace is not Merck. It is the story of Jesus. The help that comes to us only from Jesus by his self-giving love. And all of this is for our flourishing.

SWIMMING IN THE NEW STORY OF GRACE

In Scripture there are many different angles or themes from which we can glimpse the multi-faceted nature of God's grace through the gospel. We'll spend some time exploring these themes.

It has been said that the gospel is shallow enough for a child to wade but deep enough for an elephant to swim. In other words, the gospel is simple enough to be believed in a moment of time by someone with elementary intellect—yet the depth and richness of the gospel cannot be mined exhaustively even by those who devote their entire life to it's study.

Each member of the Trinity extends grace to us in a distinct fashion.

- The Father grants us unconditional acceptance.

---

[18] Michael Useem. *The Leadership Challenge*. NY: Three Rivers Press, 1998. 10-42.

- Jesus cleanses us from sin and inseparably unites us to himself.
- The Holy Spirit energizes and empowers us for life with God.

There are many different angles, or themes, from which we can glimpse the multi-faceted nature of God's grace through the gospel.

It is an immeasurably tragic belief to presume that we've attained a comprehensive understanding of the Kingdom of God. At that point, discovery dies. Wonder for salvation slowly suffocates. But this isn't necessary. Because the Trinity is the content of the message of the Kingdom, we have infinite pathways of exploration to journey down—each of which leads to a fresh view of what God has done for us through Jesus.

We might say we "know" aspects of Jesus' life and mission. We must let our hearts and minds travel these familiar paths. But certainly there is more of Jesus to be discovered and re-discovered. So we must also explore less worn paths in the same forest.

Like a diamond the work of Jesus is multifaceted and shines uniquely from different angles as we hold it up to the light. Here are some of those facets.

Jesus is Our Substitute

Before becoming a dad, I remember conversing with a friend about something he had attempted with his son. It was a radical effort to provide his young son's mind with a tangible picture of grace.

After repeated disobedience, it was time for Carlos to experience the consequences of his actions. Discipline was called for. Trevor sat with Carlos and explained how he had earned a spanking. Trevor then raised the wooden spoon in judgment, and cracked it twice on his own thigh.

Trevor became a substitute for his son. The judgment that Carlos deserved, was both inflicted and absorbed by his father.

When it comes to our sin, God could not simply withhold judgment. Sin causes real pain, brokenness, and suffering. The pain must land somewhere. It must be absorbed by someone. Jesus willingly became that someone. At the cross, he became our substitute.

Probably the most familiar theme of the atonement (the word used to describe what Jesus accomplished through his life, death, and resurrection) is "penal-substitution." Jesus died for our sin, in our place.

Isaiah 53 states this prophetically: "He was bruised for our iniquities and punished for our transgressions. The punishment that brought us peace was upon him."

Or as Paul says in 2 Corinthians: "God made him who knew no sin to become sin for us, so that we through him, might become the righteousness of God." Some have called this truth "the great exchange"—our sin for his righteousness.

The Father Adopts Us Because of Our Union with Jesus

The adoption process is a legal transaction with legal ramifications. Parents have to go through the legal transaction, applications, paperwork, meeting with people, possibly going before a judge, and then eventually having the names and identity of these children transferred. Whatever their names were before, that changes once they come into the new family. The adoption process between God and a Christian is somewhat similar.

Since before God created the world, you have been loved by God. If you have responded in trust to his love demonstrated through Jesus, you have been chosen by him. There was a moment in your life where your eyes opened to the reality of Jesus. God gave you the gift of faith and enabled you to believe. By believing in Jesus, there was a legal transaction that occurred. You have been justified. Not just declared "not guilty" but declared "righteous" in the sight of God.

Yet there is still so much within you and I that does not resemble the Father who has adopted us. The discrepancies highlighted by our perverse motives and desires can easily drive us to either despair or to hide. Our thoughts and feelings condemn us. But the Father does not.

He pulls out the adoption paperwork. He reminds us that we've been united to Jesus and are secure because of him—not because we independently live up to the family name. And then the voice of the Holy Spirit, who was placed within our hearts, who has sealed our hearts, who now indwells us—begins to point us to Jesus. He reminds us, "You belong to the Father because you are in Jesus."

Our eyes turn from objections and insecurities regarding our personal insufficiency and we are silenced by the perfection of Jesus, in whom we stand.

Jesus says us, "You didn't choose me; I chose you first." Through Christ, God chose you to be a part of his family. Satan would love to convince you that:

- "You don't belong to God."
- "God isn't real."
- Or perhaps more common, "God is all that he is—but not to you. You have disqualified yourself from his family by your sin."

None of that is true. You have been adopted and you are his forever. John tells us, "Even if our hearts condemn us, God is greater than our hearts for he knows all things."

God Reconciles Us to Himself Through Jesus

You and I could write a romantic-comedy together. The same recycled plot points tick like clockwork. Yet the stories of blossoming love still capture us when they are well done.

One of those predictable plot twists is "the misunderstanding" or "the offense." The truth comes out, "I did ask you out as part of a dare—but then I really fall in love!" Or false assumptions are made, "I saw you laughing with that other girl!" When the viewer knows "the other girl" was just a cousin.

Just as the relationship takes off, everything hits the fan, bringing the future of the couple into serious question. At this point in the film, we long for a restoration of what was broken. We believe this relationship *ought to be*. We want to see things repaired through a confession, an apology, or a mediated conversation.

This longing is a longing for reconciliation. And history is the tale of a severed romance between God and humanity. Imagine watching it unfold before you in a theater. God creates us for himself. We dwell in paradise together, enjoying each other, conversing together, creating together. Then "the offense." After "the offense," humans forget about their lover and content themselves with distractions. All the while we're weeping in our seats screaming, "What are you doing? Go back to the one who loves you! You're supposed to be together."

Despite what *ought to be*, humanity doesn't want God. If restoration of this broken relationship is to happen at all, it will only happen through God.

Paul explains in Romans, "For if while we were enemies we were reconciled to God by the death of his Son, much more, now that we are reconciled, shall we be saved by his life" (Rom. 5:10). Later he writes: "God was in Christ reconciling the world to Himself" (2 Cor. 5:19).

Without the intervention of Jesus, we are dead, heading for dead-er. In Luke, Jesus is conversing with a man about following him. The man says, "I need to go bury my dad." (Most scholars believe the man's father was not yet dead.) And Jesus replies, "Let the dead, bury their own dead." In other words, let those who dabble in death deal in death. Let those who operate day-to-day in spiritual death, bury those who have now physically died.

Death is a departure of that which ought to be united. Death is separation. At the cross, Jesus tastes physical and spiritual death—separation from the Father—so that we don't have to. For a moment, the Trinity was rifted so that we could come to experience the life of God. Because of this moment, we can be reconciled to God.

Jesus is Our Redemption

A story of redemption will always whisk the listener into an account of torturous bondage, incredible danger, and bold deliverance. The greater the reversal of fortunes in such an account, the greater the act of redemption.

God's daring rescue of sinners through Jesus is the greatest story of redemption ever conceived. Ultimately, no reversal of fortunes is more significant. Nor could there ever be a more powerful redeemer who effects the deliverance.

> Say therefore to the people of Israel, 'I am the Lord, and I will bring you out from under the burdens of the Egyptians, and I will deliver you from slavery to them, and I will redeem you with an outstretched arm and with great acts of judgment. – Exodus 6:6

The Exodus is the paramount example of redemption in the Old Testament. Yahweh frees Israel from slavery in Egypt by ripping them from the cruel grip of Pharaoh and he does so because of his promise to Abraham (Gen. 12:2).

The Hebrew roots *pada* and *ga'al* are used in varying forms to describe redemption both in the Exodus account and throughout the Old Testament. After the Exodus, God gives the law and builds the practice of *ga'al* into Israel's familial structure.

You may have read about the "kinsman-redeemer" laws in the Old Testament. The closest male relative was obligated to redeem relatives in distress. The *go'el* would buy family members back from slavery (Lev. 25:48-52), cover the debt of their mortgaged property (Lev. 25:25-34), execute justice by avenging one who killed a relative (Num. 35:19), or marry a widow in order to produce family offspring (Ruth 2:20).

The writers of the New Testament develop the theme of redemption through the latest and greatest act of the story—the cross and resurrection.

In Mark 10:45, Jesus states that he did not come to be served but to serve and to give his life as a ransom for many. There are plenty of popular thrillers where the good guy is forced to pay an enormous price to kidnappers in order to "buy back" the one that they love. As entertaining as these movies are, the best illustration for ransom and redemption remains the Exodus account—not the Greek slave market and certainly not scripts acted out by Mel Gibson (*Ransom*) or Denzel Washington (*Man on Fire*)!

This distinction is significant because the stories we connect to "ransom" influence our understanding of why Jesus had to die a sacrificial death for our sin in our place. If the blood of Jesus is a precious ransom price (1 Pt. 1:18-19) to whom was Jesus' blood paid?

Without the lens of the Exodus, some might mistakenly believe Jesus was the ransom price paid to Satan by the Father. In this scenario, somehow Satan negotiates his demands and the death of Jesus was the cost he required. However, the cross is not some sort of hostage negotiation between God and Satan. Properly understood, the cross is a spiritual and eschatological re-enactment of the Exodus. Yahweh wrests his chosen people from the hands of an evil ruler—no negotiations. The ransom price that was paid is a price determined according to the eternal plan of the Trinity. The Father, Son, and Spirit do not appease Satan at the cross. Rather, the Father and the Son partner together to pay the ransom, which appeases the wrath of the Father and the Son against sin.

The authors of the New Testament also bring further clarity to the categories of redemption established in the Old Testament.

In relation to future redemption from our bodies and from death, Paul quotes Hosea 13:14 and then builds upon the concept:

> When the perishable puts on the imperishable, and the mortal puts on immortality, then shall come to pass the saying that is written: 'Death is swallowed up in victory. O death, where is your victory? O death, where is your sting?' The sting of death is sin, and the power of sin is the law. But thanks be to God, who gives us the victory through our Lord Jesus Christ. (1 Cor. 15:54-57).

Through the cross, Jesus has redeemed us from sin. Through the resurrection, Jesus has redeemed us from death.

As it pertains to deliverance from sin, Paul tells Titus that we have been redeemed from lawlessness (Titus 2:14). He explains to the Galatians that we are redeemed from both the curse of the law and the sin that the law exposes (Gal. 4:5). As a result we are free from bondage to sin and alive to God through Jesus. We are also adopted into the family of God.

The redemption accomplished by Jesus is the ultimate expression of the grace of God which brings us into right relationship with himself and allows us to be credited as righteous (Rom. 3:24, Eph. 1:7, Col. 1:14).

Jesus is the ultimate kinsman-redeemer of the Old Testament law. He has truly become our redemption (1 Cor. 1:30). By him we are marched out of the kingdom of darkness and into the kingdom of God. We are no longer helplessly held in bondage to sin and Satan but delivered into the kingdom of light. The story is one of unimaginable reversal. From bondage to freedom. From death to life. From darkness to light. From sin to righteousness. From helpless to hope-filled. From enemies of God to children of God.

Jesus is Our Victor and Our Triumph

If a Roman commander in chief won a complete victory over the enemy on foreign soil, and if he killed at least five thousand soldiers and gained new enemy territory for the Emperor, that commander was entitled to a Roman Triumph. The commander would ride through the city on a golden chariot surrounded by officers. The parade would also include a display of the spoils of battle as well as captive enemy soldiers. Roman priests would follow behind and carry burning incense to pay tribute to the victorious army and to Jupiter. As the priests burned the incense the odor meant different things to different people. To the enemy it meant death because they were being taken somewhere public to be mauled by wild beasts. To the army it meant life and victory and celebration.

There are some amazing similarities between the Roman Triumphs and the Ultimate Triumph of Jesus because of the cross. Colossians 2:14-15 tells us that at the cross, Jesus publicly disarmed the rulers and principalities of this world and put them to shame by triumphing over them. So Jesus went into enemy territory and won an eternal victory through the cross and through his resurrection. You and I are like the spoils of battle that Jesus rescued from enemy territory. At the same time, we are also like the army that is returning with Jesus from the battle and as Romans 8 says, "We are more than conquerors through him who loved us."

What exactly has Jesus triumphed over?

- Jesus defeated Satan and his demons by eliminating their grounds for accusation (Rom. 8:1, 31-39).
- Paul describes the cross as a public shaming of Satan (Col. 2:13-15).
- Jesus triumphed over death through the resurrection and promises resurrection to believers (1 Cor. 15:55-57).
- Jesus conquered our sin and all that was due to us because of our sin (Rom. 8:2).

Jesus is Our Propitiation and Expiation

The film *The Prestige* begins with a monologue describing the nature of all good illusions:

> Every great magic trick consists of three parts or acts. The first part is called "The Pledge." The magician shows you something ordinary: a deck of cards, a bird or a man. He shows you this object. Perhaps he asks you to inspect it to see if it is indeed real, unaltered, normal. But of course... it probably isn't. The second act is called "The Turn." The magician takes the ordinary something and makes it do something extraordinary. Now you're looking for the secret... but you won't find it, because of course you're not really looking. You don't really want to know. You want to be fooled. But you wouldn't clap yet. Because making something disappear isn't enough; you have to bring it back. That's why every magic trick has a third act, the hardest part, the part we call "*The Prestige*."[19]

---

[19] "The Prestige – Quotes. IMDb. Accessed February 12, 2014. http://www.imdb.com/title/tt0482571/quotes

As the monologue rolls, Cutter (played by Michael Caine) chooses a small bird from among a room full of identical birds in identical cages.

The same monologue is used to conclude the movie as well and shows Cutter performing the "bird trick" for a young girl. This illusion is illustrative of the entire plot and is performed throughout the movie as a subtle message to the viewer.

First, a bird is presented and then placed in a cage. The bird and the cage are then placed on a table and covered with black cloth. The magic happens when the cage folds up flat and collapses, thus "disappearing" into the cloth. This kills the bird placed in the cage. The trick finishes with the appearance of an identical bird, playing the role of the first bird. It takes two birds to perform the trick.

It is almost as if someone meditating upon the sacrificial instructions in Leviticus 16 invented this illusion. Here Moses describes the annual Day of Atonement sacrifice.

Two unblemished goats were chosen. The priests then cast lots for which role each goat would play.

The first goat was laid on the altar, prayed over by the priest then slaughtered. This was intended to communicate the truth that without the shedding of blood there can be no forgiveness of sin (Heb. 9:22).

The second goat was also prayed over. The priest confessed the sins of the people and they were symbolically transferred to the goat. The creature was then set free out into the wilderness. God commanded this ritual to teach Israel, "There go your sins. Gone with that goat."

The Day of Atonement sacrifice illustrates two true facets of Jesus' atoning work on our behalf—propitiation and expiation.

Propitiation is a payment, typically a sacrifice, that turns away wrath. You're probably familiar with how this plays out in mythology.

In Greece, people might have said, "Look at this lightning. Zeus is angry. Let's make a sacrifice."

The Christian understanding of propitiation is both similar to and different from this sort of view. It is similar in that, when we are born into the world, our status is "children of wrath."

Those of us who are more conscious of our moral deficiencies observe the pervasive brokenness within our lives. We think, "Look at my selfishness. God is angry. I'll make a sacrifice."

We attempt to effect some kind of propitiation for our sins. But 1 John 2:2 describes how the wrath of God against sin has been turned away from us: "He [Jesus] is the propitiation for our sins."

Unlike in pagan propitiation, God makes a sacrifice through Jesus that we could never make to appease his own wrath. Jesus is the bird crushed in the cage; the goat slaughtered on the altar absorbing the wrath of the Trinity into himself.

Jesus is also like the second bird and the second goat. Jesus accomplishes expiation through his atoning work.

Expiation is the canceling of sin. The psalmist describes the essence of expiation beautifully when he writes that God has separated our sins from us as far as the east is from the west (Ps. 103:12).

The funny thing is if you travel north long enough you'll hit the North Pole and then begin traveling south. Not so with the east and west. Start traveling east from Seattle and you'll move through America, reach the Atlantic, travel through Europe, Russia, Japan, the Pacific, back through America, to the Atlantic. You can travel both east and west infinitely.

Through Christ, God has separated our sin from us as far as the east is from the west. The east and the west will never meet. That second goat that's been released into the wilderness is gone and he took our sins with him. That's expiation.

Jesus is the Restorer of Culture

Jesus does not just help sinners, he helps those who have been sinned against. What does the work of Jesus mean for the daughter whose dad beats her? How does Jesus offer hope to victims of sexual slavery in Thailand? What word does Jesus speak to citizens oppressed by tyrannical governments?

These people are not only individual sinners, they are victims of sinful systems. Thankfully Jesus not only saves us and will save us from our individual sins but saves and will save us from systemic evil. The redemptive ministry of Jesus extends into culture.

We need an atonement that covers the full scope of sin. If you believe that sin is only individual, you will proclaim redemption that covers only individual sin. But when we begin to see that sin is also systemic, we uncover the need for an atonement that is larger in scope. Thankfully the atonement is big enough to cover both individual and systemic sin.

In *When the Kings Come Marching In*, Richard Mouw exposits Isaiah 60 as a day when the Messiah (Jesus) will heal and restore culture. Mouw writes, "A political reckoning must occur and this will be a public event in the city."[20] Sinners cannot just hit and run. Judgment will fall on the leaders who facilitated evil governments and systems.

When Jesus sets up his kingdom on earth, the cultural tools and resources that were used to rebel against him will be redeemed and re-oriented around him to display the radiance of God.

As we enjoy Jesus and announce him to others, we must think bigger. The work of Jesus is multi-faceted in its brilliance. We must never limit the work of Jesus to one particular angle. The person and work of Jesus must not be condensed in order to ease digestion. The more robust our view of Jesus, the more robust our understanding of the kindness of God will be.

GRACE CAN RE-WRITE THE STORY YOU LIVE

Paul says, "I am what I am by the grace of God" (1 Cor. 15:10). He's saying, "Everything I am today is a product of the way God continually gives himself to me."

---

[20] Richard J. Mouw. *When the Kings Come Marching In: Isaiah and the New Jerusalem*, rev. ed. Grand Rapids, MI: Wm. B. Eerdmans Publishing Co., 2002. 57.

Elsewhere, Paul told the Romans, "It is the kindness of God that leads us to repentance" (Rom. 2:4). In other words, when we begin to grasp the way God offers himself to us—when we really "get it"—we enter his embrace. We turn from lesser loves and enter a shared life with him. That has always been God's desire for humanity. To invite us into the joy of shared life with God. Jesus makes that possible.

Jesus destroys the notion that I am valuable or lovable because I have gifts and try to do stuff with them. Instead, the Bible teaches that we are significant because we are united with Jesus and have now been adopted into God's family. What I do or don't do is not transactional currency in the Kingdom of God. The only currency God accepts is the work of Jesus accomplished on our behalf. This is grace. It is true and available. And it is better than any of the false stories we're living.

THINK

- How would you describe the quality of "grace" to someone else?
- What facet of grace seems most stunning to you as you consider this conversation?

LOVE

- Grace either softens us or hardens us as we are exposed. Spend some time praying through the response you desire for yourself.

DO

- Consider who might benefit from what you're learning about Jesus and the grace that he has become for us. How might you humbly and helpfully share some of this in a way that would benefit them?

OUR SECURE PLACE IN GOD'S STORY
Conversation 6

Solomon Northup, an African-American freeman during the 1800's, made a living for his wife and two children as a violinist in Saratoga, New York. In 1841, slavery was legal in the South but not in the North.

Through a series of deceptions, Solomon was drugged and kidnapped. The recent movie *12 Years a Slave* depicts Solomon waking up on a cold cement floor in chains just a few miles away from the nation's capital. After a few hours agonizing in his chains, a man enters the room. The man inquires about Solomon's name and identity.

As Solomon begins to explain his family back in Saratoga and his status as a free man, the man throws him to the ground and begins to beat him shouting, "You're a slave, you're a Georgia slave. Are you a slave?" When Solomon says, "No." The beating continues. This evil slave trafficker intends to whip the identity of freedom out of him.

You and I face a similar spiritual struggle as Solomon Northup. For those of us who belong to Jesus, God declares us free. Yet there are voices and pressures that would love to beat our identity out of us. We're all facing a battle between slavery and freedom and what's crazy is you may not be what you think or what you feel.

Your life and actions are a product of your perception of your identity. In other words, you act according to who you *be-*

lieve you are. Are we sinners or are we saints? Are we some sort of strange hybrid? If we are saints then why do we so often sin? If we are merely sinners then what affect has the work of Jesus really had? How can I desire so earnestly to obey Jesus yet so consistently deny him with my actions? If I have a new nature then how can I have a sin nature?

Without careful consideration, we will lose our identity when the whip strikes. Conflict will disorient us. Our own sin will pressure us to believe that *maybe* we are somehow a "Georgia slave." And if we lose trust that we have a secure identity in God's story, we are teetering on the edge of a dark abyss.

YOU ARE UNITED TO JESUS THROUGH TRUST IN HIS WORK

Union with Jesus is indicated throughout the Scriptures by the tiny preposition "in." The phrase refers to the fact that we participate in the life, death, and resurrection of Jesus by faith. Romans 6:1-12 is one of the clearest explanations of this doctrine in the New Testament. Put simply, those who have placed their trust in Jesus are now united with him in every way possible. We are inseparably linked to Jesus in such a way that his life becomes our life, his death has become our death, his resurrection has become and will become our resurrection, and his glorification will be our glorification. Chronologically, some of this has already taken place in the past tense—at the moment we first trusted in Jesus. Some of it remains a future promise.

We share in the death of Jesus.

When Jesus took your place at the cross, he was dying to kill a cancerous part of you: your old man. Biblical authors, Paul in particular, are abundantly clear that are old man was put to death on the cross. As surely as Jesus experienced the wrath of the Father against sin at the cross, and, as surely as, Jesus died at the cross, your old man also died. As a result, Paul exhorts us to "Reckon yourself dead to sin" (Rom. 6:11). Within the ritual

of baptism, sharing the death of Jesus is pictured in the moment
, Christians are submerged beneath the surface of the water just
as Jesus was in the tomb.

We share in the resurrection of Jesus.

The same Holy Spirit that raised Christ from the dead has now
given us life. Although our bodies are still subject to disease,
decay, and death, the Holy Spirit who lives in us is a deposit, a
foretaste, and a guarantee of the fact that physical death is only
a temporary condition. Disease and decay may be part of our
existence right now, but they certainly will not be when the
Kingdom of God is established on the earth. Within the act of
baptism, the Christians shared resurrection with Jesus is pictured the moment we rise up from out of the water just as Jesus
emerged from the grave after three days. "We were buried
therefore with him by baptism into death, in order that, just as
Christ was raised from the dead by the glory of the Father, we
too might walk in newness of life" (Rom. 6:4).

We share in the life of Jesus.

In order to say "yes" to anything in life, you must say "no" to
something else. Every decision you make in the direction of a
certain lifestyle requires the slow death of another sort of life.
The same is true of our life with Jesus. As we follow him, we
must allow false and twisted parts of ourselves to die in order to
truly live in the footsteps of Jesus. For this reason Paul writes, "I
am crucified with Christ and yet I live; Not I, but Christ that
lives with in me" (Gal. 2:20). Elsewhere, amid the extreme hard-
ship of ministry, Paul further explains this strange correlation
between death and life: "Always carrying in the body the death
of Jesus, so that the life of Jesus may also be manifested in our
bodies. For we who live are always being given over to death
for Jesus' sake, so that the life of Jesus also may be manifested
in our mortal flesh. So death is at work in us, but life in you" (2
Cor. 4:10-12).

We also share in the life of Jesus by having the same mind. Several passages (most notably 1 Corinthians 2 and Philippians 2) describe how we share the same mind as Jesus. These authors aren't stating that we actually have the same physical brain as Jesus. The writers of Scripture mean we have the same Holy Spirit which informed the thoughts and will of Jesus now residing within us, guiding our lives if we hear and obey as Jesus did.

We will share in the glory of Jesus. The resurrection of Jesus is not only an event that verifies his divine and messianic identity. The resurrection of Jesus is significant because Jesus is the first person death could not keep in the grave. Jesus' work now makes it possible for a new humanity to share in his conquering of death. Jesus says, "I am the resurrection and the life. He who believes in me will never die" (Jn. 11:25).

But how do we reconcile the teachings of Scripture with the clear reality that the bodies of many Christians currently lie lifeless six feet under ground? Part of the answer lies in the truth that there is more than one sort of death. One death separates man from God. This is spiritual death. Another death separates man's soul from body. This is physical death. The final death separates man from God eternally. This is eternal death.

On the cross, Jesus tasted separation from the Father as he absorbed the wrath of the Trinity against sin. We are now saved from separation from God and immediately delivered from spiritual death. In doing so, Jesus also saves us from eternal death.

Children of God who died today find their souls immediately in the presence of God. Nevertheless, the soul is separated from body and physical death is still a reality. However, when Jesus returns to establish his kingdom on earth he will physically resurrect his people. Souls that belong to God will once again become embodied. The only difference is that these bodies have no susceptibility to sin, disease, or death. These bodies are what the Bible calls "glorified" (1 Cor. 15:40, 53). We will then live forever with God in bodies like Jesus. We will share in the glory and joy of Jesus as we experience his kingdom here on earth.

THE FATHER CREDITS YOU WITH THE RIGHTEOUSNESS OF JESUS

A long time before Jesus came to earth, God revealed himself and made some incredible promises to Abraham. God commanded Abraham, "Leave your homeland and go to a place I will show you. I am going to make a great nation out of you. By you, everyone in the world will be blessed." Abraham never saw these promises completely fulfilled. By the time he died, Israel was not a great nation. Israel was not a nation at all.

Although the promise seemed dead at times and Abraham's trust suffered prolonged spasms of doubt and fear, Abraham oriented his life around these promises. Through that belief in God's promises, he was credited with righteousness.[21]

Likewise, when we respond to Jesus in trust, we are credited righteous before God just as Abraham was. Scripture refers to this new status as *justified*. Although formerly identified as "children of wrath," "enemies of God," and "slaves to sin" (Eph. 2) responding to the gospel gives us a new status. We become "children of God" who are covered by his grace and his righteousness. We are legally declared righteous before God, and our sins are no longer counted against us.

The implications of this new status are enormous. It means that our status with God isn't dependent upon our performance. Obeying God's way doesn't earn us his approval or improve our status. Conversely, disobeying God's way doesn't tarnish our standing with him. But something in us finds this hard to swallow. As a result, many people see their status with God as something dependent upon them. They either live in pride and self-righteousness when things are going well or they live in guilt, condemnation, and doubt when they succumb to temptation. For this reason, Martin Luther once said, "I preach justification by faith to my congregation every week. Because every week they forget." May we not forget that the security of our status

---

[21] See Genesis 15:6, Romans 4:1-12

with God lies in the finished work of Jesus, not on our shoulders.

THE SPIRIT GIFTS YOU WITH A RIGHTEOUS HEART

Imagine living on the streets. All your earthly possessions fit inside a weather-beaten backpack. You struggle to stay alive. No source of income. No reliable shelter. No food outside of what you can scrounge up. But you've been homeless for so long that's just the way life is. It seems normal.

You stand in a crosswalk one day and a limousine pulls up beside you. The door pops open and an unfamiliar face says, "Come in." After confirming your schedule is open, you shrug your shoulders, sling your dusty backpack onto the luxurious leather, and take a seat.

"We're headed to a party and thought you might want to come along." Within a few minutes, the car rolls up to a security checkpoint. The guard peers skeptically through the drivers window into the backseat. His eyes fall upon you. "Any credentials for that one . . . " The stranger seated with you in the back chimes in, "They're with me, don't worry about it." The security guard nods and waves the car through but you can't help but feel a little uneasy about being here.

"This is the biggest house I've ever seen," you mutter as you follow your mysterious party-friend through the majestic entryway. While the outside of the home was immaculately white, the inside of the home floods your eyes with lush reds and regal blues. This doesn't make sense. "Hang on a minute . . . " The stranger turns their head and slows the pace only slightly, followed by a "Let's keep on, keeping on."

You seem to arrive at the entrance to the party. Through the double doors everyone is well-dressed and dining on fine foods you didn't know existed. There's just one thing between you and this ridiculous party . . . 350 pounds of man. This bouncer looks mean. "He's with me," your friend assures. "I don't care whose with who no one gets in dressed like that! Get . . . "

You wait for the rest of this sentence to drop, but it never does. Your ticket to the party shushes the bouncer and removes their watch and their shoes as they push you through the threshold to the room. They place the watch on your wrist and replace your hole-ridden sneakers with their exquisitely fashioned footwear. A young woman with a scrumptious cheese platter drifts within reach and you scarf down the better part of the appetizers she's carrying. You smile in cheese-full bliss and she smiles back as if she understands that you're new at this whole unlimited cheese thing. "Welcome to the White House," she offers as she departs to replenish her platter.

Fun story, right? The idea of being relocated from poverty to luxury is an appealing one. And we can probably all relate to riding someone's coattail into a place that we wouldn't have ordinarily been accepted. Who wouldn't want a backstage pass to the concert or a VIP status to stand on the sidelines during the big game?

Many people imagine our relationship to God in such a way. "Jesus picks me up off the street and takes me to the Father. I can go to the party because I'm with him (union with Jesus). I can get into the party because he covers me with some of his fancy righteousness and I'm good to go (justification)." That's a pretty good story. But there is an important theme that's missing from the picture: transformation. Not only does Jesus take us to the party and clothe us in his righteousness, we actually become different people on the way there.

Regeneration describes how the Holy Spirit actually performs a heart transplant on us when we trust in Jesus. Our old heart is replaced with a new one. This new heart has new desires and a new nature. Our core identity actually shifts. We become different people. No longer does Jesus say to the Father, "She's with me." By the work of the Spirit, Jesus can also say, "She is now like me." Through this miracle, we become "partakers of his divine nature" (2 Pt. 1:4). What exactly does that mean?

YOUR CORE IDENTITY IS NOT "SINNER"

Ephesians 2:1-3 describes the impoverished state of a human being without Jesus.

- We were dead. Although we were created by God and for relationship God, we have become separated from him as a result of sin. Our status is 'spiritually dead'.
- We followed the world and Satan. Paul is basically saying, "The course of your life and your guiding passions are a result of the influence of Satan and your slavery to sin."
- God was righteously wrathful towards us. Paul's point here is: "You are disconnected from the God who gives meaning and significance to life, and apart from him your passions are misdirected, hollow, empty, and destructive to you and others. God's mad about that."

As if that weren't bad enough, two chapters later (Eph. 4) Paul further describes the identity and function of people who don't know Jesus in these ways:

- **Darkened in their understanding**: Our thinking has been darkened and disabled by sin. Paul mentions this elsewhere like in 2 Corinthians 4 where he says, "Our gospel is veiled to those who are perishing because in their case the god of this age, Satan, has blinded their eyes to keep them from seeing the light of the gospel—Jesus." In 1 Corinthians 2 he talks about how spiritual truths cannot be interpreted and understood by someone who doesn't have the Holy Spirit.
- **Excluded from the life of God because of ignorance**: The word "ignorance" sounds pretty harsh but it simply means that there is a lack of knowledge or someone is uninformed. The one who has not believed in Jesus is separated from God as a result of their lack of belief.
- **Hardness of heart**: I've sometimes found in my conversations with people outside the faith that people have an

"intellectual" objection to the faith. We then talk about their objection and resolve it. But they still won't believe. Because that intellectual objection isn't really the problem—a hard heart is. It's important to remember that many times people don't reject Jesus for intellectual reasons but for heart reasons.

- **'Given themselves up to ___'**: Before Jesus you are enslaved by your sin. All of who you are is tainted. This doesn't mean that every single thing you do is sinful, but it does mean sin is the default tendency and it does mean you are defined by your sin.

In the verses that follow (Eph. 4:20-24), Paul transitions and begins talking about the identity of one who has believed in Jesus.

There are some important phrases here: "old self," "former manner of life," "new self, and "created after the likeness of God."

When Paul mentions the "old self" here, the term means the same thing as the "old man" in Romans 7. The old self is the identity rooted in sin, right? Now if you understand that then there is a problem with this verse. Paul seems to have his chronology wrong!

If you are a Christian your "old self" (your identity rooted in sin) is already dead and gone. So why in the world does he say to put it off? If its already dead in the past tense then why put it off in the present tense?

Star Wars Episode V: The Empire Strikes Back begins with a giant blizzard on the planet Hoth. In order to stay alive Luke uses his light saber to slice open a camel-like creature and crawl inside. The scene is pretty disgusting really. I can't imagine crawling into a dead carcass. But what if you liked the warm comfort? What if you started living life in that carcass? You went to work in it, ran on the treadmill with it, ate in it, watched TV in it. Seem strange and bizarre? Not only is it nauseating but it's ridiculous, unnecessary, and irrational. Yet it's exactly what many of us are doing with our identity!

The reason Paul says put off the old self when the old self is already dead is because some of us are dragging around the burden of our old identity. It's almost as if you are dragging around a carcass! Your old identity rooted in sin (the "old self") is an unnecessary burden you drag around when it has nothing to do with who you are.

When Paul says to "put on the new self" he is not telling us to get saved again. The new self is already an internal and spiritual reality that has taken place. "If anyone is in Christ he is a new creation. Old things have passed away and all things have become new" (2 Cor. 5:17). What Paul is saying is that we need to presently put on our identity. In your thinking, you need to understand that the 'new self' is the reality of who you are.

If you are a Christian you are not the same person you used to be. The very core of who you are has changed. Your identity rooted in sin has been replaced with what verse 24 describes—an identity created after the likeness of Jesus in righteousness and holiness.

I want to examine two implications of this truth. They are closely connected. First, your core identity isn't: "sinner." Second, sin is a violation of your identity not a confirmation of it.

Obviously sin is still something we do, but it is now in conflict with our identity. Before Jesus our identity was rooted in sin and we functioned accordingly. Now our new identity is rooted in Jesus and his righteousness—that's the truest part of who you are—but, if you still think of yourself in "old self" standards then you won't function according to your new identity.

In other words, when we think of ourselves primarily as filthy sinners, we will function accordingly. When we grasp the fact that we have a new-self created after the likeness of God, trust in the Father's acceptance, remember our union with Jesus, and rely on the Spirit's strength we will also live accordingly.

At times following Jesus seems like an exercise in pretending. We may feel we don't really belong in the family of God but we'll "fake it til' we make it." But following Jesus isn't about pretending. It's about becoming who we are. It's about finding ourselves invited into the joyful and secure life of the Trinity because of Jesus. It's about embracing our new status and new place in his family and abandoning the way we used to exist.

It's about breathing in the breathtaking grace of God and receiving it with celebration. The Father now calls us righteous because of Jesus. The Spirit imputes the righteousness of God within us. And we are "in Christ," secure in the love and acceptance of God.

FOUR FUNCTIONAL IDENTITIES OF A JESUS-DISCIPLE

How do these realities of our new righteousness and new identity play out functionally? How will these truths manifest themselves practically in the life of a disciple? Here are four functional identities of a Jesus-Disciple. They are "identities" because they describe our new hard wiring, but they are also "functional" because they involve tangible activities which are played out as we follow Jesus and seek his Kingdom.

1. Storyteller

As we discussed in Conversation 1, each one of us orchestrates our life to follow along with some kind of big story. A disciple of Jesus is one who allows their head (knowledge), heart (soul, will, emotions), and hands (actions) to become increasingly shaped by God's story of redemption through Jesus. We discover this story through the Scriptures.

Storytelling is something inherent to our humanity. We are wired for story, learn through story, and inevitably tell stories. Followers of Jesus tell a story about a true and better way of life—the Kingdom of God.

2. Worshipper of God

We have also discussed how we are by nature worshipping beings. That is to say we are always desiring, wanting, or pouring ourselves out to something or someone. A disciple of Jesus asks God to change what they most deeply want (because we cannot change what apart from the Spirit), so that their worship is increasingly redirected to God.

On a daily basis, we find ourselves betraying the good God who loves us perfectly. We find ourselves living for false loves believing that they can give us something God cannot. Our worship is like oil dumped into a cracked funnel. It spills out and is wasted. Yet the Father accepts us because we are "in Christ" even when we are faithless, Jesus is faithful. When God whispers such kindness and forgiveness to us, it ought to lead us away from false stories and false loves and back into the story of the Kingdom.

3. Restorers

We believe that Jesus will return again to set up his Kingdom here on earth. At that point, God will abolish sin, injustice, pain, oppression, disease. As citizens of God's Kingdom we are to use our talent, skill, and passion to give people a glimpse of what the Kingdom of God is like. That means we have the joyful opportunity to join God in the renewal of all things. Each one of us has an opportunity to help the world taste the Kingdom by being a *restorer* and participating with the ultimate Restorer—Jesus.

4. Disciple-Former

Jesus has asked us to give ourselves to the work of teaching others his way of living and being. He has equipped us for this task through sending a Helper—the Holy Spirit. So we are to both "be" (in the sense of walking out our identity) and to form disciples of Jesus. We are to help others along on the same journey we travel. A journey where our head, heart, and hands are increasingly transformed by the helping power of God.

OUR SECURE PLACE AS DISCIPLES UNDER JESUS

A few months ago I started learning how to make sushi. Thankfully, the ingredients are tasty enough that no matter how poorly I build a sushi roll I can still enjoy the taste. It is ridiculously hard to make sushi the right way.

In Japan, a sushi chef takes about ten years to earn the title of chef. They have a "master" who teaches them certain skills and then gives them space to improvise and innovate on certain techniques.

I was recently in a discussion with some friends about what it means to be a disciple of Jesus. Someone brought up that discipleship is not so different from the training process they have for sushi chefs in Japan.

One of the big similarities is a simple one: both take a really long time. One sushi chef says, "I have made sushi for 29 years, and I am still learning."[22]

May we never stop learning under Jesus. We may slice our fingers with those sushi knives. We may serve people badly mangled sushi. We may want to give up and cry at times, but that's all part of being a disciple. Thank God that we aren't kicked out of the family for our ineptitude.

May John the Beloved's words assure you that you also are secure and beloved of God, "See what kind of love the Father has given to us, that we should be called children of God; and so we are...for whenever our heart condemns us, God is greater than our heart, and he knows everything." (1 Jn. 3:1, 20)

You are a child of God. Feelings of condemnation don't change that status. God is greater than your feelings and your failures. And through Christ, he has secured a place for you in the grand story he is weaving.

---

[22] Jacques Lhuillery. "It Takes Years to Perfect the Art of Making Sushi - Business Insider." *Business Insider*. February 5, 2013. Accessed April 17, 2015.
http://www.businessinsider.com/it-takes-years-to-perfect-the-art-of-making-sushi-2013-2#ixzz34TWSjOAe.

THINK

- How would you describe your new identity "in Christ"?
- What functional identity of a Jesus-apprentice do you feel most drawn to? Which identity stirs the most fear inside you?

LOVE

- What do you sense the Spirit saying needs to shift in your heart as a result of this conversation?

DO

- Engage a friend or family member surrounding the ideas we've discussed in this conversation that are most meaningful to you. To kick-start a conversation on "identity" consider asking them, "What is it that makes you, you?"

MAKING GOD'S STORY VISIBLE
Conversation 7

Wes Anderson's film *Moonrise Kingdom* unfolds on the small island of New Penzance. For residents, life is predictable and safe. As viewers meet key characters, we see flashes of the loneliness and insecurity that they've hidden. But two twelve year-olds, Sam and Suzy, have found something more—each other. Sam, a boy scout, uses his wilderness survival skills to run away with Suzy. They create their own little kingdom that stands in contrast to the status quo of the island. Their community of love alerts others to the truth that a different way of living is possible.

Christians are citizens of an alternative, spiritual, invisible kingdom. But submitting to our invisible King makes his kingdom a little more visible to those who are not yet citizens. As we begin to live in freedom, others come to witness the freedom of his Kingdom.

All of this means that the Kingdom of God is not something we build, make, fight for, push for, or help God with. Instead, "Always, everywhere, the kingdom is a gift we receive, a Presence we enter, a reality we inhabit. Jesus is the kingdom."[23]

[23] Leonard Sweet. "Comments." Facebook. January 26, 2014. Accessed April 17, 2015.
https://m.facebook.com/story.php?story_fbid=10151844469051791&id=583321790.

As we live into the true and better way of Jesus our lives begin to appear different. For our friends, family, and neighbors the sensation is like being led to a window. Through the window is a scene they've been searching for all their lives—the Kingdom of God.

THE UTOPIA THING DOESN'T WORK

While a community of love and togetherness is cute on film, I can't help but wonder if it is really possible. My skepticism isn't just a grouchy pessimism. It's often rooted in the pain of past experiences.

It certainly doesn't help that the word "community" has been hijacked as a rallying cry for faith-based organizations, neighborhoods, and even banks like the one by my house. It is difficult for any ideal to maintain its semantic integrity when it has become so diluted in its usage.

The experience of community might be even more disorienting than the word itself. Your experience might feel like you were headed in for a hug, but somehow the collective leg of the community was raised and kicked you where it hurts. Whether the kick was accidental and clumsy or targeted and malicious is not always a reassuring confidence booster for attempting the same hug all over again. The church isn't exempt from these pains.

Perhaps part of the problem is the unspoken assumptions we have about the essence of life in community. As leaders, the common vision we rally people around is, "This will be great. Let's do 'life together.' Let's eat together. Let's share our possessions." (or however it is said by the leadership) A relational utopia is advertised—often in a way that allows me to accessorize my individual self—but this only sets people up for disappointment and disillusionment.

But what if the wounds we give and receive aren't antithetical to the possibility of a community of love? What if our collective woundedness actually opens the door for communion with

God and community with each other? What if the perfection of community isn't demonstrated through our sinlessness but through our confessing, repenting, forgiving, and reconciling? What if we told people, "Hey welcome to a church family where we hurt each other sometimes. Where we both sin and are sinned against. What makes this a beautiful, Jesus-born community is the fact that we want to practice grace with each other when those things happen. That means confronting and confessing. Rebuking and repenting. Forgiving and being forgiven. Receiving and extending grace."

The utopia thing doesn't work. When we add a dose of biblical realism to our recipes for community we can say to others, "You are welcome with us here. We aren't the perfect community. But you are being invited to participate in the life of the perfect community—the Trinity. Your craving for a perfect community is a longing for the Trinity."

WOUNDEDNESS IS THE WAY TO COMMUNION AND COMMUNITY

Our individual and collective woundedness is reality. To fail to acknowledge our pain and our sin forces us to live within a lie—an alternate reality. Embracing reality makes it possible for us to experience the Kingdom of God, communion with God, and community with each other.

Last year I sat with a dozen young men as they confessed their deepest shame and hurts to each other. Some were caught in addictions. Others were victims of abuse. All of them had been wounded by others and wounded others by their own actions. As we bore our souls to each other, people began to weep. Prayers for one another poured out for hours. It was a taste of heaven on earth and we all knew it.

During his thirties, Jean Vanier bought a house in Paris and invited three developmentally disabled men to live with him. That was half a century ago. Since then, Vanier has formed and lived in similar communities. In *Community and Growth* he writes, "I am struck by how sharing our weakness and difficulties is more nourishing to others than sharing our qualities and successes."[24] He then suggests that love involves seeing a person's gifts and their wounds.[25] This is, in fact, how God sees us. Part of loving others well means helping them to see these things within themselves. Rarely are we conscious of the depth of our pain or the depth of our gifts.

Our hearts shrink from giving and receiving this type of love in community. Vanier explains why, "Love makes us weak and vulnerable, because it breaks down the barriers of protective armour we have built around ourselves. Love means letting others reach us and becoming sensitive enough to reach them."[26]

What does this look like practically? The human experience, our relationships, and community life . . . all of it centers on a journey towards love. Vanier writes beautifully on the nature of the journey:

> We believe that the Father loves us and sends his Spirit to transform our hearts and lead us from egoism to love, so that we can live everyday life as brothers and sisters.[27]

Of course, as we live everyday life with others, the experience often adds to our frustration, confusion, guilt, and pain. But it is this story of God's love that opens up the possibility of relationship and community. The history of love begins with God. God is, within himself, a community of perfect love. There are portraits of community being sold everywhere. But only those portraits that are sourced in the ultimate reality of the Father, the Son, and the Spirit are portrayed with clear vision.

---

[24] Jean Vanier. *Community and Growth*, 2nd ed. NY: Paulist Press, 1989. 185.

[25] ibid, 43.

[26] ibid, 48.

[27] ibid, 312.

GOD IS COMMUNITY

"Fourth Century theologians painted a picture of God that they hoped would give people a vision of what it would mean to fellowship with God, to enjoy the experience of communion with him. They came up with the word *peri-choresis,* which literally means to dance around—*peri* means around, as in perimeter, and *choresis* is from the same root as choreography. The Trinity, they suggested, could be properly envisioned as dancing together in the perfect rhythm of love at a wildly exuberant party."[28]

Being created in the image of God means that without understanding God we cannot properly understand ourselves. We must discover the God we share common ground with in order to grasp our blueprint and our function. God tips us off to this early on—laying all his cards on the table. When God creates Adam and Eve, he says, "Let us make man in our image, after our likeness" (Gen. 1:26). Is it a coincidence that God reveals this mysterious plurality within his nature as he breathes the human race into being? God is community, and our ability to participate in his story is only possible when we pursue community.

The Trinity Points to the Human Need for One Another

When God made the heavens, the earth, and all of his creation, he was satisfied and said it was good except for one thing. "It is not good for man to be alone" (Gen. 2:18). We are social and relational beings because we were made in the likeness of a social and relational God. Not surprisingly, Christians are given countless New Testament commands to avoid being alone. It is still "not good" to be alone. The people of God are supposed to

---

[28] Larry Crabb. *Soul Talk: the Language God Longs for Us to Speak.* Nashville, TN: Thomas Nelson, 2005. 225.

gather together regularly (Heb. 10:24) and run the race of faith together (2 Tim. 2:22). The New Testament is famous for the phrase "one another"—indicating the impossibility of orthopraxy (right practice of the faith) without others. The story of the gospel can only be practiced in a community context.

In Matthew 28, Jesus tells the disciples to baptize new disciples in the name of the Father, the Son, and the Holy Spirit. We may think of baptism only as a signal of identification with the death and resurrection of Jesus as Paul teaches in Romans 6. But baptism is more than identification with Christ—it is identification with each member of the Trinity. It interesting that being baptized into identification with the Triune God—who exists in perfect community—coincides with our birth into another new community, the church. From this point on, we need never think of ourselves in isolation.

The Trinity is our Model for a Community of Unique Roles

Throughout church history, theologians have not only understood the Trinity to be ontologically Trinitarian but also economically (functionally) Trinitarian. What in the world does that mean?

God is not one essence of three persons who all do the same thing in the same way. The Father functions as the creator, sustainer, and ruler; the Son as the mediator, Messiah, and redeemer; the Holy Spirit as the helper and the one who testifies of Jesus. 1 Peter 1:1-2 teaches that each member of the Trinity participates uniquely and is necessary in God's salvation plan.

Imagine the Father saying to Jesus, "I don't need you anymore." Of course, that is unthinkable. Paul says the exact same thing of individual members in the Body of Christ. It would be unthinkable for a "hand" to say to a "foot," "I have no need of you." In the church, we must understand that the diverse functions and roles which individuals members have are mutually supportive. We need each other so that the church can work together properly and build itself up in love. Similarly, the Trinity is the church's model of a community of diverse roles that each function to build itself up.

It should be noted that the Trinity does not build itself up in the sense that it progresses, changes, or grows. The Trinity does build itself up in a different sense though. The Son came and testified of the Father. The Spirit comes and testifies of the Son. The Father now exalts the Son and will exalt the Son for eternity. So the building up in love occurs for the purpose of mutual and shared glorification, not growth in love.

The Trinity Reveals the Vitality of Mission for Community Life

Being baptized in identification with the Trinity also means being baptized into identification with the Trinitarian mission. God's heart is that none would perish but that all would come to repentance. Jesus connects the redemptive mission of the Trinity with the community of believers in his prayer to the Father: "As you sent me into the world, so I have sent them into the world" (Jn. 17:18).

The idea of a perfectly loving and fully joyful community reaching outside itself for any mission seems counter-intuitive. Yet that's exactly what the Triune God does. Many human-formed communities are exclusive. But Jesus is overwhelmingly enthusiastic about the disciples sharing in the intimacies of the Trinity. He prayed, "Father, I desire that they also, whom you have given me, may be with me where I am, to see my glory that you have given me because you loved me before the foundation of the world" (Jn. 17:24). The privilege of enjoying relationship with the Triune God and enjoying relationship with the people of God is not some elite frequent flyer club. Everyone is invited to the party although not everyone responds.

It is fascinating that most authentic community does not exist to enjoy itself forever, but embarks together on a mission to reach outside of itself. There is no true community without mission. As a result, if we want to truly participate in life with God then we must adopt his mission.

Alan Hirsch, missiologist and writer, articulates the distinction between community and *communitas*. Most Christian community or fellowship exists for the sake of itself. However, *communitas* is the sort of community that is formed when a group shares a common purpose and mission. Through the shared risk, adventure, and even fear—they move forward and create a depth of relationship that is not possible otherwise.[29] The church is to be this kind of community. Our mission is making God's story visible to the world and inviting others to participate. How does the church go about this mission in the real world?

THE CHURCH IS A COLONY THAT MAKES GOD'S STORY TANGIBLE

God's purpose has never been to make the world a bit more Christian. His purpose in this age is to create a people who are living in the world system, but operating under an entirely different rule, order, and allegiance. In this age, those people are the church. In the age to come, he will fully establish his Kingdom on earth and completely eradicate all other false ways of living.

At a primal level, it seems the church understands we ought to be about some kind of social transformation in our world. But how we channel this social activity and the sort of change we hope it will bring about is vastly different. At the risk of generalizing this complex question, I have tried to depict two differing (Christian) strategies for social transformation (*see graphic on page 119*).

I am not suggesting Christians should abstain from voting and political involvement. In fact, in Conversation #9, we'll see how the opposite is true. The question here is simply this, "Where does our hope rest? What are you trusting in for redemption and restoration?"

---

[29] Alan Hirsch and Debra Hirsch. *Untamed: Reactivating a Missional Form of Discipleship (Shapevine)*. Grand Rapids, MI: Baker Books. 2010.

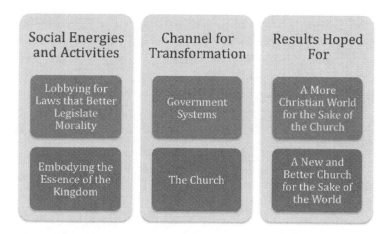

Social Energies and Activities	Channel for Transformation	Results Hoped For
Lobbying for Laws that Better Legislate Morality	Government Systems	A More Christian World for the Sake of the Church
Embodying the Essence of the Kingdom	The Church	A New and Better Church for the Sake of the World

This all flows back to our Creation-Brokenness-Redemption-Restoration story framework. If you believe that the fundamental brokenness of our country is that not enough people vote Republican (our Brokenness), then you will always be trusting the next great candidate for Redemption that will bring about the Restoration you imagine.

I hope that you can see the brokenness of that story. Whatever our political involvement is to look like as Christians (again, wait for Conversation #9), we must remember that the ultimate hope of our world does not rest in the outcome of the next election. Our hope rests in the fact that Jesus is King. Whatever faulty judgments are rendered by our courts—Jesus will judge good and evil in the end. Whatever immoral laws may be legislated, we are subject to a higher authority—the ethics of the King and his Kingdom.

Vanier explains his belief about the political significance of Jesus-centered communities:

> Some Christians are very taken up by politics. They can be terribly anti-communist, forming rather fascist organizations to fight the 'red devil'. Or they can be fiercely anti-capitalist, fighting for new structures and redistribution of resources. Both these tendencies can lead to a centralization – whether to protect the free market economy or to further wholesale nationalization.

I sometimes wonder whether these fighting Christians wouldn't do better to put their energies into creating communities which live as far as they can by the charter of the Beatitudes. If they did this, they would be able to live by, and measure progress by, values other than those of material success, acquisition of wealth, and political struggle. They could become yeast in the dough of society. They would not change political structures at first. But they would change the hearts and spirits of people around them, by offering them a glimpse of a new dimension in human life – that of inwardness, love, contemplation, wonderment, and sharing.[30]

As God re-writes the stories we live, the transformation is evident. The plot changes and we change with it. We are set free from the guilt and shame that would drive us away from the Father. We are unchained from the compulsion to impress the Father to earn acceptance and belonging. We are released from trying to fix ourselves and control our lives. We have the liberty of free decision in matters not specifically addressed in the Bible. We are free from the dark powers that used to deceive us. More than this, we hold fast to the sure hope that our world will be free from systemic evil, oppression, violence, abuse, and injustice. When Jesus establishes his Kingdom, we will be free from the effects of sin, disease, death, and suffering and we will be free to relate to God and others with incorruptible love.

This is the story that can change the world. More than that, this is the story that *will* change the world.

So how does a community root themselves in this story and express it in a way that makes sense to others?

---

[30] Vanier, 308.

A COMMUNITY ROOTED IN THE STORY OF GOD

As some Israelites returned from exile, Ezra and Nehemiah restoried the people of God (Neh. 9). Once the people heard the story they made specific commitments to God.

Even today, the story of the Kingdom requires an adjustment in our daily practices and rhythms. Of course, these practices do not justify us before God. They do not earn us his grace. Instead, they are designed to keep us in steady remembrance of God's justifying grace.

The Bible doesn't provide a tidy list of approved practices. It seems that in every unique cultural context the Holy Spirit sparks creativity for the expression of the Faith—but always in a way that is true to the story of the Kingdom and which speaks prophetically to the surrounding culture.

Adelphia is a one-year discipleship experience for young adults. It is the community where I live and lead. We have a list of nine specific practices that we believe serve this purpose for our students. By no means is our list comprehensive or even fully translatable to another context so I won't share all of them. However, I do believe that in Western contexts, these practices confront many of the false narratives and false loves of our culture, while forming our students in the way of Jesus.

1. Share Meals

As we live in the Kingdom, meals become an experience of grace, community, and mission. Tim Chester has argued that how we eat actually reflects our personal vision for life.[31] If this is true, then a Kingdom vision should bring a Kingdom flavor to our meals.

---

[31] Tim Chester's *A Meal With Jesus: Discovering Grace, Community, and Mission Around the Table* has been extremely formative for me on this subject. It was not until reading this work that the significance of shared meals and the kingdom became apparent to me.

Following in the footsteps of Jesus, we should attach great significance to who we eat with, cook for, make time for, and dine with. These things say everything about our mission in life. So the everyday rhythm of meals is an opportunity to further the mission of forming disciples of Jesus. Furthermore, the future Kingdom will include delicious food and drink. We ought to allow that feast-filled future to leak into our present.

2. Remain Grounded in Scripture

Scripture is the primary channel through which God reveals his essence and character, his redemptive purposes, and his will for our lives. Similar to the experiences of both Ezekiel and John in Scripture, in a sense, God is asking us to "eat this book." That means we chew on the story of God. We derive nourishment and energy from the story of God. We digest the truth and it becomes part of us. This process may look different in different contexts but the goal is the same—remain grounded in Scripture.

3. Undistracted Presence

A wealth of research on social media and entertainment has emerged. No matter the source, the research consistently points out the ways in which media can actually diminish our quality of life. Rather than being fully present in a particular moment and place, we disintegrate ourselves by engaging in a digitally constructed pseudo-reality.

No matter how ordinary or mundane the simple moments of life might seem there is a divine soundtrack playing softly behind it all. Yet too often, we miss this experience because we have headphones on. Or we're binging on Netflix. The need for noise, the obsessive compulsive craving for incessant entertainment, our social media usage—these practices actually say something about our hearts if we are willing to listen.

Never before in history has the practice of "choosing embodiment" been more counter-cultural. That's not an overstatement either. If we adopt this practice, it will be a prophetic witness to our culture and it will certainly help keep us aligned with God's bigger story.

4. Sacrifice and Serve

Scripture tells us that the greatest demonstration of love imaginable is the substitutionary death of Jesus on the cross for our sin. If the story of the cross is what forms our understanding of love then we might define love as the willingness to suffer for the shalom of another.

Our culture abhors performing menial tasks that are not applauded or recognized by others, are not fun, may be boring, and don't directly contribute to our personal vision for success and happiness. Adelphia includes opportunities for this kind of sacrificial service precisely because it is so difficult. Something dark in us is aggravated by such work. In that moment of aggravation, the Holy Spirit invites us to a conversation of repentance and transformation.

5. Be Silent

Blaise Pascal, theologian and philosopher, writes, "All of humanity's problems stem from man's inability to sit quietly in a room alone." It may be an overstatement to suppose that our root problem is the inability to sit in solitude. Perhaps our intolerance for solitude is a symptom of our deepest brokenness. What are we afraid of discovering when we are alone in our self-reflection? What might the Holy Spirit say to us in such a moment? What vulnerabilities, façades, and insecurities might be exposed if we hit pause on life in order to consider the way we were living?

INVITE THE SPIRIT TO GIVE YOU CREATIVITY FOR NEW EXPRESSIONS OF THE KINGDOM IN YOUR CONTEXT

The practices above are simply examples and aren't comprehensive. Walter Brueggeman suggests that an alternative community in Western society would involve these three practices: hospitality, generosity, forgiveness.[32] That would be quite a start towards cultivating a Kingdom community. In a culture of rampant individualism, may we serve others in our homes. In a culture of materialism, may we live generously and sacrificially. In a culture full of suffering and pain, may we extend the forgiveness and grace of Jesus.

So, how will you participate with God to help others see his story in our world? Use the Think/Love/Do questions below as a starting place for cultivating communities with the DNA of the Kingdom.

---

[32] Brueggemann, Walter. "An Alternative Way." The Work of the People. Accessed February 8, 2014.
http://www.theworkofthepeople.com/an-alternative-way

THINK

- What would be different about a community that displayed the true story of the Kingdom?

LOVE

- What false loves need to die inside you so that you can cultivate community that reflects the heartbeat of God's Kingdom?

DO

- Sketch out a list of practices that you think might help you live out the story of the Kingdom and give others a window into the life of the Kingdom. Choose 1-2 of those that are most important right now, and create a plan for moving forward. Share your plan and why this is important to you with someone that can offer support.

EXPLORING OUR LANDSCAPE
Conversation 8

It's been subtle, but the American Dream has mutated. Oftentimes the subtler a change, the more important it turns out to be. Neal Gabler describes this morphing in a piece for The Boston Globe:

> The American Dream, as it was devised in the late 19th century, referred to opportunity. The idea was that anyone in this pragmatic, un-class-conscious society of ours could, by dint of hard work, rise to the level of his aspiration.
>
> But over the past 50 years, the American Dream has been revised. It is no longer about seizing opportunity but about realizing perfection.[33]

This new ideal shows up just about everywhere in Western society. Lexus is "passionately pursuing perfection." Before and after testimonials promise that life will be so much more livable with product XYZ. The ideal of perfection is also reflected in what we don't see on meticulously photoshopped magazine covers.

---

[33] Neal Gabler. "The New American Dream – the Boston Globe." *The Boston Globe*. March 31, 2011. Accessed April 17, 2015. http://www.boston.com/bostonglobe/editorial_opinion/oped/articles/2011/03/31/the_new_american_dream/

Our culture flawlessly disciples us into this ideology. We are sold these stories of perfection which actually stir desire in us. These stories paint a picture of the way the world is supposed to be—and we want this picture to become reality in our individual lives.

The pursuit of perfection isn't all bad though. It is partly true, partly exaggerated, and partly a lie. Is there a way my world ought to be? Certainly. But the source for this vision of *oughtness* matters greatly.

Twenty years ago, Michael Warren foresaw the way in which mass media would shape our vision for life and drive consumer culture.

> With the prevalence of electronic communications, especially electronic story-telling, everyone, including youth, has unlimited access to compelling, acted-out versions of reality, vivid imaginations of what life is all about. In consumerist capitalism many of these imaginations are part of a strategy for orchestrating consumption.[34]

I don't think it is an exaggeration to state that some people derive their definition of love from *The Notebook* or some other romantic film (or maybe *Star Trek*. . . you never know!) The point is, whether or not we realize it, movies are an example of how cultural goods stir imagination within us for how life ought to be. They shape our beliefs, give definition to our values, and fuel our hopes. Many films spend millions of dollars to draw out specific emotions and pull you into a new reality for a couple hours.

I'm not suggesting you boycott the movie theater or vandalize billboards in a zealot-like rebellion against culture. I am simply observing—with the helpful insights of great thinkers who have observed before us—that there are deep undercurrents pulling us in directions we may not even be aware of. Our

---

[34] Michael Warren. "Cultural coding and ecclesial re-coding in the young." St. John's U, Part 2, *Youth, Culture and Religious Community, Gospel and Our Culture 6:3*. Sep 1994.

culture and the goods it produces are designed to move us towards a precise response.

These realities make it impossible to press into the way of Jesus without considering the ways we are already being shaped by our world and examining the dynamics of our cultural landscape. So let's explore.

WHAT IS CULTURE?

Nature is what God created. Culture is what humans created from what God created. "Culture fulfills the latent promise of nature. To echo biblical language, the egg is good, but the omelet is very good."[35]

We don't really "make" culture. It would be more accurate to say we make the goods, products, artifacts, and services that cumulatively contribute to culture.

Andy Crouch, executive editor at Christianity Today and writer, helps define culture in this way: "Culture is what we make of the world. Culture is, first of all, the name for our relentless, restless human effort to take the world as it's given to us and make something else."[36]

The restlessness we feel to create is a result of our human hardwiring. Because we are made in the image of an imaginative Creator, we feel a compulsion to reflect that likeness. Before the fall, God commands Adam and Eve to put effort into creating. This command has come to be known as the *cultural mandate* or the *creational mandate*. God asks humans to harness the wild beauty and power of nature and to subdue it for the purpose of fruitfulness.

Of course, the fall has changed the reasons humans create cultural artifacts. We have distorted ideas of beauty. We abuse resources for selfish gain. We maintain our *imago dei*, but it is hugely marred by pervasive sin.

---

[35] Andy Crouch. *Culture Making: Recovering Our Creative Calling.* Downers Grove, IL: IVP Books, 2008. 31.

[36] ibid, 23.

We are already familiar with the idea that a person's ultimate love sets the trajectory for their life. This pursuit of "the love" is unmistakably a pursuit of meaning. During this pursuit of meaning, an individual will create and make that which they believe will best contribute to the Kingdom of their Ultimate Love. Crouch writes, "We make sense of the world, by making something of the world. The human quest for meaning is played out in human making."

Our vision for life and what it ought to be (meaning) leads us to create, innovate, produce, and act. The college frat dude who thinks up some new drinking game innovates out of his love for the party life. The scientist who devotes her life to testing and experimenting is driven by the hope of eradicating cancer. We are always creating and contributing to the kingdom we love.

CULTURE'S STORIES ARE SHAPED BY THE CULTURAL LANDSCAPE

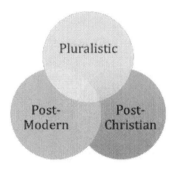

Pluralistic

According to pluralism, there is no universally accepted story for understanding truth and ultimate reality. We all live according to very different stories since there is no one dominant religion in our world.

"In modern western culture, so Berger argues, we are all required to be heretics, for there is no accepted plausibility structure. With respect to ultimate beliefs, pluralism rules, and thus each individual has to make a personal decision about ultimate questions. In that sense, we are all now subject to the "heretical imperative."[37]

Post-Modern

The essential characteristic of postmodernism is a skepticism about certainty. It argues against any single system of objective truth. "It [postmodernism] has produced a self devoid of intrinsic value and without a social reference for significance. The postmodern individual, a consumer of endless products marketed primarily on the basis of image and style, has aestheticized all of life, rendering it flat in texture and undifferentiated in meaning."[38]

The aestheticization of all of life leads to an accessorizing of the individual self in order to find meaning in self-expression. Since we can't be certain of meaning in anything—in any one universal source—meaning is given to everything.

Post-Christian

In describing Western society's relationship with the gospel, Lesslie Newbigin writes, "It is a pagan society, and it's paganism, having been born out of the rejection of Christianity, is far more resistant to the gospel than the pre-Christian paganism with which cross-cultural missions have been familiar."[39]

---

[37] Lesslie Newbigin. *Foolishness to the Greeks*. London, UK: SPCK, 1986. 11.

[38] Hunsberger et al., 132.

[39] Newbigin, 20.

Mark Driscoll observes the state of Christianity in America: "There are more left-handed people, more Texans, and more pet cats then evangelicals in America."[40]

ENGAGING CULTURE

It is no secret that the church in our part of the world is struggling. When and where did the Western church slide off the rails? On the whole, the church failed to contextualize the message of the Kingdom to our present cultural context. By *contextualize* we mean the particular way the good news about Jesus is communicated and embodied in our culture. We told a story that was incoherent.

The gospel is not tied to any particular culture, so it shows up as good news in different ways to different people groups because it critiques and confronts different cultures in different ways. Here's what the process of contextualization looks like typically. It begins with knowing the stories of a given culture.

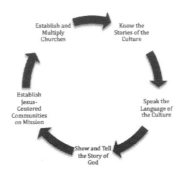

---

[40] Driscoll also writes, "Common statistics estimate that evangelicals represent anywhere between 40 to 70% of the country's total population, where approximately 130,000,000 people. However, more extensive research cited by John Dickerson in his book the great Evangelical recession indicates that the actual ranges between seven and 8.9%, somewhere between 22 and 28 million people. Moreover, all studies indicate that younger people are less likely to be evangelical."Mark Driscoll. *A Call to Resurgence: Will Christianity Have a Funeral or a Future?* Carol Stream, IL: Tyndale, 2013. 13.

The Church's ability to engage culture redemptively hangs on our ability to faithfully move through this cycle. Moving forward will require at least five deep shifts in our current practice.

1. Shift from "the culture" to "our culture"

In John 17, Jesus prays that we would be in the world. Modern Christians may be surprised to know that this is not a prayer we need to work at to accomplish. We are already in the world. We are already shaped by the stories and ideas of culture. Properly engaging the culture begins with understanding that we both contribute and participate in that same culture. Culture is not somewhere *out there*. The culture is in us.

What we have failed to recognize is that the gospel's first order encounter with the culture we inhabit will be with us, not with any of *them* out there.[41]

What does this mean practically for cultural engagement? It means that the best means for evaluating how the gospel will break into our culture, is by examining our own hearts. (Thus the need for us to engage the sort of prophetic practices we talked about in Conversation #7)

Almost inevitably, the barriers to the gospel that exist in our own hearts are a product of the culture we have grown up. Therefore, the barriers to the gospel that Jesus exposes in our hearts, are identical to the barriers of the gospel in our culture. This is so because "the culture" is actually "our culture."

2. Shift from Cultural Frustration to Cultural Intelligence

Andy Crouch identifies several potential postures towards culture. Each of these postures is characteristic of particular pockets of the Christian faith in America: condemning, critiquing, copying, and consuming. These are appropriate cultural gestures in a given cultural situation. However, when condemning,

---

[41] Hunsberger et al., 295.

critiquing, copying, or consuming become the default postures with which we consistently interact with culture that is a problem.

Each of these approaches to culture could be considered cultural engagement, but only in a generic and superficial sense. It is a mistake for Christian who blogs negatively about government legislation and the current US president (critiquing) to think that he is helpfully and redemptively engaging culture. Rather than contributing to change he is simply offended by what is happening.

Another posture is copying. It is an oversimplification for a church to think that they can become culturally relevant by rivaling the entertainment value of the family fun center down the street. This posture may also explain how the Christian music industry has emerged.

Others simply consume what culture produces—no questions asked. In some churches, this posture may earn you the title *relevant*. However, it is deluded to believe that pop culture references and keeping up on the latest happenings in the sports world are the epitome of relevance. Real relevance only occurs when we are cultural fluent.

We are indeed responsible to engage culture and that requires cultural fluency. Cultural fluency is much deeper than any of these postures mentioned above. Cultural fluency requires examining the epistemological (the branch of philosophy that examines how we know what we know) foundations that serve as the bedrock for our cultural beliefs.

Culture is more about what's under the surface than what is in the headlines. Culture is as much about what we're blind to as what we can see. What is in the headlines gives some glimmers of culture's "fundamental presuppositions," but it takes more work than just reading the headlines to have a complete grasp on them.

3 x 7 = 20. Of course, we know that's not true. How? We memorized the correct answer in school. But what if this was the answer we had memorized? What if this was the answer that everyone had memorized?

In a manner of speaking, culture assumes some answers are wrong. We are told that some answers don't add up. It is extremely difficult to critically identify them, but with some work we can. For the Christian, probing the areas of our heart that are not yet submitting to the reign of God can often help identify some of the "bad equations" we have accepted from our cultural upbringing.

At one point a friend asked me, "What do you want most in life?" I answered quickly and instinctively: "To be secure." In so many ways, my life is a pursuit of the desire for security. But does the answer I am pursuing "add up"? I feel a compulsion to save more money, earn more money, accumulate more money—and it is tied to my desire for security. I am a disciple of American capitalism. I really do need to be rescued from the broken story that money equals security.

When the church is fluent in our own culture and in the good news of Jesus, we will have a true missionary encounter with Western society. Only when we understand the "bath math" embedded within our culture, can we speak the good news of the gospel to our society. It is at this point that we become truly culturally relevant. As Tim Keller says, "Christianity must make emotional and cultural sense before someone will consider if it makes logical or rationale sense."[42] Cultural fluency, not frustration, helps us tell the story in a way that makes sense to those around us.

3. Shift from a Minimalistic Gospel to a Holistic Gospel

This minimalistic gospel was the result of a modern strategy for evangelism. Altar calls seem to be the result of the belief that a preacher could deliver the salvation message and immediately called for a decision. This is indeed true at times. But the idea seems to have been that an encounter between the information

---

[42] Gabe Lyons shared this quote during his lectures to Dr. McKinley's Doctor of Ministry cohort in June 2013.

of the gospel with the human mind was all that was necessary for conversion. Presentations of the gospel were then reduced to the lowest common denominator. In an effort to make the gospel more mobile and portable its legs and arms were cut off. It's like showing someone a two-minute trailer and then asking, "Is this your favorite movie now?" Whether they say "yes" or "no" they haven't heard the whole story.

The *movie trailer* presentation of the gospel might sound something like this, "You are a sinner. Jesus came to die for your sin on the cross. If you believe in him you can be forgiven and go to heaven when you die."

The trailer axes a discussion of our origins and design. We were created in the image of God. Such a presentation also neglects an understanding of the Kingdom that is now and not yet (which is imperative to participate in the kingdom here and now). Any sense of mission is bypassed. Such a gospel is individualized to the point that any meaning in community is peripheral and unnecessary. It's a truncated story.

Truly if the church is to engage culture meaningfully in Western society, we must shift from offering a minimalistic story to the world and instead provide a holistic and compelling story of redemption.

4. Shift from Evangelism as Decision to Discipleship as Life in the Kingdom

The painful but accurate perception is that Christians are insincere and concerned only with converting others.[43] There are deep mutations that have occurred within evangelicalism. These mutations have created an obsession with "making decisions for Christ." Now a strange distinction exists between evangelism and discipleship. These changes have actually formed a new definition of discipleship.

---

[43] David Kinnaman and Gabe Lyons. *unChristian: What a New Generation Really Thinks About Christianity... and Why it Matters*. Grand Rapids, MI: Baker Books, 2007. 67.

People don't embrace Christianity because of intellectual arguments. In fact, *rational thought* can easily lead us away from God in many cases. John Piper talks about this in *Think: The Life of the Mind and the Love of God*. The Pharisees were super smart. But their hearts were evil. So their intelligence was hijacked and corrupted. Only those who love rightly, see rightly. What ends up saving us is not logic, but love.

Deeper paradigm mutations have occurred which led to evangelical preoccupation with conversion. Within the last hundred years, a false dichotomy between evangelism and discipleship has emerged. We think evangelism is for unbelievers and discipleship is for believers. But really, both are for both. To avoid the confusion, it is probably easiest to refer to discipleship as the aim of our relationships. We are discipling people in the way of Jesus and the way of the Kingdom. And this doesn't have much to do with conversion. Someone can follow Jesus and appreciate Jesus before they understand his Messianic identity.

In many ways, I've observed a correlation between the length of time that someone takes to decide to follow Jesus and the perseverance of their decision. I've observed a young man come to Jesus in sixty minutes through the altar call of a charismatic pro athlete. I've preached messages to people who make the decision after I invite them to "pray a prayer." But these people didn't embrace the Kingdom and begin to live in it.

When it comes to discipleship—whatever we draw people with is what we will keep them with. If we draw them with emotionalism and entertainment then that's what it will take to keep them involved in the community and our flavor of "discipleship." If we win someone with a decision they make in one hour, then we should expect their decision to withstand about one hour of spiritual combat pulling them away from Jesus.

For all of these reasons, conversations about "conversion," "accepting Jesus into your heart," "making decisions for Jesus," and even "evangelism" are inadequate. At the very least, these must become sub-categories of a larger discussion: discipling people into Jesus and his Kingdom. This takes much, much longer than converting people. This involves plenty of uncharted gray areas, volatile, unscripted conversations and relationships, and much more time than asking someone to convert. *This is discipleship. This is what Jesus has commanded us to do.*

5. Shift from Church Growth to Kingdom Participation

We need local churches that care more about participating in the Kingdom than in growing their church.

Bob Roberts, author and pastor, highlights the distinctions between disciples of the church and disciples of the kingdom of God. This table indicates how disciples of the church and samples of the kingdom of God think differently on these four issues.[44]

	CHURCH	KINGDOM
Gospel	Salvation	Kingdom of God
Disciple	Information	Hear and Obey
Society	Ignore	Engage
Church	Building	Movement

Practically speaking, it seem many churches are concerned with the question "How can we get people into the church building?" A better question is, "How can we participate in God's Kingdom work in the neighborhood?" Rather than praying, "God please bring all the people you want to come," we must pray, "God please lead us to the people you want us to disciple."

---

[44] Roberts shared this view during his lectures to Dr. McKinley's Doctor of Ministry cohort in June 2013.

INVITE THEM INTO ANOTHER WORLD

Michael Warren writes, "Religious traditions have a powerful antidote if they will invite their people, including the young, to enter an alternative world of meaning enriched by a deeper human imagination than that of the consumerist society."[45]

As we inhabit and explore our culture we are simultaneously called to proclaim and embody the Kingdom. To help them imagine an alternative way of living—the way of Jesus. Living and inviting others into the true and better story of the Kingdom doesn't require less imagination. It requires more.

---

[45] Michael Warren. "Cultural coding and ecclesial re-coding in the young." St. John's U, Part 2. *Youth, Culture and Religious Community, Gospel and Our Culture 6:3*. Sep 1994.

THINK

- Where does culture seem to grasp for meaning? Remember, if making is the pursuit of meaning then the most widely appreciated cultural goods give us an indicator of the meaning people are looking for.

LOVE

- In what ways are you a disciple of culture? How do you think Jesus wants to confront and give you freedom from this lie with his grace?

DO

- Experiment. For the next couple days as you watch commercials, make coffee, and consume cultural goods, take a step back and ask the question, "What is the 'good news' story this thing is preaching to me?"
- Revisit the practices you sketched out in Conversation #7. Now that you have some added perspective on our culture from Conversation #8, revise, add, subtract, and improve the practices you would like to cultivate. Remember, these practices are to keep you in the story of Jesus while serving as a counter-cultural witness.

IMAGINING THE KINGDOM
Conversation 9

In 1973, two Princeton researchers conducted what has come to be known as the "Good Samaritan experiment." A group of seminary students were individually instructed to prepare a speech on the story of the Good Samaritan.

After filling out some questionnaires, some people were told they were late to deliver the speech in a nearby building. Other subjects were told they had plenty of time.

> Along their path to the other building an actor was slumped over and groaning, pretending to be sick and in need of help. Of the seminary students who had plenty of time, about 60 percent stopped and helped. The ones in a rush? Ten percent helped, and some even stepped over the actor on their way.[46]

Jesus both proclaimed and embodied the Kingdom of God. If that's how Jesus communicated the message of the Kingdom it's probably a good model for us too. Think about how the Good Samaritan parable and the experiment warn us of our nature. We often miss the chance to embody the Kingdom while we are rushing to proclaim the Kingdom somewhere else.

---

[46] David McRaney. *You Are Not So Smart*. NY: Dutton, 2011. 77.

THE KINGDOM IS WHERE GOD'S RULE IS WELCOMED

One might say that the Kingdom of God is a "comprehensive restructuring of life experienced by a people who are now under the rule of God."[47] This root metaphor of Jesus is a profoundly cultural one. The word "kingdom" is fraught with imagery and meaning. A kingdom shapes every aspect of civic life. Work, marriage, meals, recreation . . . all of life takes place within and is intensely structured by a kingdom.

Another helpful means by which we can frame the kingdom of God comes from Bob Roberts Jr. He describes the kingdom as: "The totality of all things God desires for the totality of all humanity."

In essence, the kingdom of God is what ought to be. The kingdom is the realization of the will of God. Sin has distorted and perverted the goodness of God's original creation. Yet the kingdom beckons it back into the reality of what it should be.

The Kingdom of God is both the content and the goal of the church's engagement with culture. "Missionary encounter with modern culture requires that we hold together basileia (the reign of God) as the content and goal, and incarnation [enfleshing or embodying], as the ultimate strategy, and listen carefully, respectfully, and compassionately to the modern world."[48]

One might imagine the kingdom of God as involving three facets: gospel, church, and culture. An ongoing three-way conversation exists between the gospel, church, and culture. The gospel can be understood as the message and power of the Kingdom. It is the message which Jesus announced during the beginning of his ministry. Jesus clearly equated his presence with the arrival of the kingdom of God. In many ways it seems the presence of Jesus is synonymous with the presence of the kingdom.

On this point N.T. Wright is helpful,

---

[47] Crouch, 138.

[48] Hunsberger et al., 75.

The whole point of what Jesus was up to was that he was doing close up, in the present, what he was promising long-term in the future. And what he was promising for that future and doing in the present was not saving souls for a disembodied eternity, but rescuing people from the corruption and decay that is a part of the present.[49]

THE CHURCH IS A TESTIMONY OF GOD'S RULE

The church can be understood as the people of the kingdom of God. During this age the church is the primary vehicle for expressing the rule of God on earth. The church testifies to an invisible government and proclaims to the culture that the rule of King Jesus is in fact ultimate.

Inagrace Dietterich writes beautifully on this point:

> The reign of God does not fall from the clouds; it is mediated historically by the eschatological calling forth of God's particular people. The rule of God presupposes a people, a people of God, in whom it can become established and from whom it can shine forth. As a kingdom people, the church is entrusted with the good news of the rule of God inaugurated in Jesus Christ, which is the salvation of the world. Its mission is to invite all humanity into the new social order found in relationship with Jesus Christ: To participate in the blessings of the kingdom, to celebrate the hopes of the kingdom, and to engage in the tasks of the kingdom."[50]

Our participation in the kingdom of God begins as Jesus brings us into union with the Father through the Spirit. The Spirit of God then begins to work through us bringing good fruit that manifests the way of Jesus to the world around us. This is

---

[49] N.T. Wright. *Surprised by Hope: Rethinking Heaven, the Resurrection, and the Mission of the Church.* NY: HarperOne, 2008. 192.

[50] Hunsberger et al., 367.

the only good we can do that really matters. We don't restore the world ourselves. We participate with Jesus as his kingdom breaks in. In this sense, the kingdom is now.

But the kingdom is also not yet. God's will for the world has not yet been fully realized. The consummation and fulfillment of God's kingdom is not yet complete. The promise of the kingdom has a still future element. We will be fully restored and glorified. We will be with God face-to-face. God will judge evil. There will be a political reckoning. God will vindicate the oppressed. Cultural goods will be repurposed and refashioned for the worship of God rather than for their abusive purposes in rebellion against God. This hope is what encourages us as we participate in the kingdom that is now but not yet.

SHALOM IS THE VISION OF GOD'S KINGDOM STORY

Becoming a kingdom citizen means we are invited to envision and participate in the creation of a new kind of social order. Rather than accepting perversions of the fall as inevitable, we can walk in the Spirit and watch the Spirit transform our life and the lives of those around us—bringing about a reality that we wouldn't have thought possible.

In Conversation 2, we introduced the Hebrew word *shalom*. Shalom is closely tied to the Hebrew concepts of justice and righteousness. Shalom is the way life ought to be. Tim Keller describes it by stating, "It means complete reconciliation, a state of the fullest flourishing in every dimension—physical, emotional, social, and spiritual—because all relationships are right, perfect, and filled with joy."

A Spirit-given vision of shalom is far more compelling than hearing rules. Rules are informative but lifeless and fleshless. Shalom is directive, life-giving, and requires seeing someone *do it*. That was part of what Jesus came to do—to show off a new way of living since people missed the point of the law. Even in the Old Testament, the law was really about helping Israel understand rightly ordered love—not helping them earn God's approval. The shalom Jesus models and makes possible is the alternative way.

JUSTICE IS INDISPENSABLE TO GOD'S KINGDOM STORY

Justice and the gospel are woven together. Justice has to do with what ought to be. Certainly the gospel brings about what ought to be. What ought to be is a life with all relationships (God, others, self, creation) well-ordered so that life is full of well being.

Chris Marshall writes, "Justice designates the right ordering of the universe, the way God intends reality to operate."[51] Therefore, justice is not a subjective and abstract philosophical concept, but an objective reality rooted in the revelation of God's character.

We cannot move far in a discussion of biblical justice without talking about biblical righteousness. The two are virtual synonyms in Scripture. Dr. Gerry Breshears describes biblical righteousness as "all relationships—God, others, self, and creation—well-ordered and flourishing. The righteous one is one who contributes to such life."

Through the person and work of Jesus (the gospel), God is bringing about what ought to be (justice, righteousness, shalom). But if this is true why do these concepts sound so foreign to the ear of the typical Christian? Why are these words so rarely associated with explanations of the gospel?

The answer lies in the theological movements of the twentieth century: the battle between fundamentalism and deviant, liberal theologies. Certain brands of liberals began to talk about the gospel only in terms of social justice and liberation rather than honestly confronting the deeper issue of personal sin. Some even began to teach that it didn't matter what "team" (e.g. Christian, Muslim, atheist) one did justice on. Doing justice "in the name of Jesus" was a replaceable part of their equation.

---

[51] Chris Marshall. *The Little Book of Biblical Justice: A fresh approach to the Bible's teaching on justice.* Intercourse, PA: Good Books, 2005. 23.

Fundamentals reacted—actually overreacted—by eliminating virtually all social justice elements in their gospel doctrine. What resulted was a highly individualistic spirituality. Some good came from this but sadly, they chopped off biblical ideas like justice and shalom.

Recovering a gospel that includes justice is essential for the church today. Contemporary generalizations would be that theological liberals talk about justice while evangelicals emphasize grace and mercy. The two are seen as mutually exclusive. However, the Bible emphasizes both! The church must re-gain a vision for the gospel of grace and justice if we are to proclaim and embody the way of the Kingdom.

Consider this statement from Chris Marshall while keeping the story of Jesus at the front of your mind: "We often think of justice and mercy as opposites. To show mercy when wrongdoing has occurred means suspending or disregarding the penalty which justice requires. Mercy thus represents a kind of injustice. But this is only the case if we think of mercy in strictly arithmetical or legalistic terms. If instead we understand justice in terms of restoring healthy relationships, then mercy is often the best way to get there. Mercy helps to bring about, rather than to interfere with, justice."[52]

The gospel we preach must include both grace and justice—they are not only compatible but closely connected. One necessitates the other. Each feeds the other.

The battle between fundamentalism and liberalism has not been the only scholastic shrapnel to damage biblical thinking on justice. A theological shift in the last decade has also created fallout in this issue that is necessary to address. Several key points within a tradition called Reformed theology have coalesced to create a problem in approaching justice theology biblically—specifically the concept of righteousness.

A high emphasis on man's total sinfulness and Martin Luther's thinking on justification has created an unintentional problem. Luther emphasized an "alien righteousness" imputed to the believer by grace through faith. This is the doctrine of

---

[52] Marshall, 37.

justification and a correct presentation of it at that (as discussed in our previous conversations).

What is glaringly absent from the Reformed tradition's dogma is an equal emphasis upon regeneration—the righteousness imparted to the believer at conversion through which they receive a new heart and new desires.

The problem with thinking of righteousness solely in justification terms is that it separates it from the Christian life by making it purely *positional.* Furthermore, righteousness is not pictured as totally alien in Scripture. In the Old Testament, Abraham is counted righteous through his believing trust, loyal love, and obedience from the heart to Yahweh. Jesus perfectly demonstrates God's righteousness. Paul says that we now have "the ministry of righteousness" (did he mean "the ministry of personal piety" or "the ministry of alien righteousness"? 2 Cor. 3:9).[53]

Why would we assume God only *credits* this righteousness to us rather than understanding it as the seed God has implanted in the believer through the new nature which he desires would manifest through working for justice and the shalom of the Kingdom? That is the ministry of righteousness—a life that advances the Kingdom in the name of Jesus by the power of the Spirit and brings shalom for the glory of God and the joy of the people. This is the message of Jesus.

BEING AND FORMING DISCIPLES THAT DO JUSTICE

Any deficiencies in our understanding of the gospel will result in deficiencies in the disciples we form. Sure enough, a story deficient in justice has produced many disciples who are oblivi-

---

[53] I want to credit Dr. Gerry Breshears at Western Seminary for helping me see the distinction in the two definitions of righteousness and how they apply in this particular passage.

ous to biblical teaching on justice and righteousness. Tim Keller writes,

> Biblical righteousness is inevitably 'social,' because it is about relationships. When most modern people see the word 'righteousness' in the Bible, they tend to think of it in terms of private morality, such as sexual chastity or diligence in prayer and Bible study. But in the Bible *tzadeqah* refers to day-to-day living in which a person conducts all relationships in family and society with fairness, generosity, and equity.[54]

Is this the vision our church has for discipleship? Or is our vision more related to spiritual disciplines and personal piety?

Marshall argues that contemporary discipleship provides a different focus for the disciple than Scripture does. Justice is not given due attention. "Justice is one of the most frequently recurring topics in the Bible. For example, the main vocabulary items for sexual sin appear about 90 times in the Bible, while the major Hebrew and Greek words for justice (*mishpat, sedeqah, diskaiosune, krisis*) occur over 1000 times."[55]

Spiritual health is not a personal matter that can be achieved in isolation and privacy. Rather, it is a matter of justice and shalom. Are we being and making disciples who bring about what ought to be in all of our daily affairs?

KINGDOM ECONOMICS ADDRESS THE FULL COMPLEXITY OF BROKENNESS

Poverty is never the result of a single cause. Yet, both liberals and conservatives have reduced the problem to a single series of causes. Essentially liberals say oppression produces poverty while conservatives say personal moral failure is the root cause.

---

[54] Keller, 10.

[55] Marshall, 23.

Both are oversimplifications although each side has a piece of the answer.

First, I will address the misconception of the conservatives. Poverty is caused by more than personal laziness or lack of family values. It takes more than industriousness to achieve financial success. Keller poses the question, "If you were born in the mountains of Tibet in the thirteenth century, no matter how hard you worked you wouldn't have much to show for it." He points out, "If you have money, power, and status today, it is due to the century and place in which you were born, to your talents and capacities and health, none of which you earned. In short, all your resources are in the end the gift of God."

It is not difficult to see scenarios in which people are oppressed and sinned against and experience poverty because of sinful systems that are in place. This is what liberals are able to see. Some of the shortcomings of their perspective are in believing that redistribution can create equality—when it will take far more than that (empowerment, training, etc.)—and in failing to see that personal moral failures are a part of the complex equation that creates poverty.

Regardless of which party is in office and whether we have more or less government we need to think in terms of kingdom economics. Mike Caba, in his talk on "Just Economics: Capitalism, Socialism, and the Bible," discusses what this looks like. His term for this economic paradigm is "saltandlightism."[56] He states, "God owns it all. You are his steward and servant with the purpose of bringing him glory. This is the biblical system of economics for the follower of Christ." The wonderful thing about this system is that it can work within any existing system or government.

It's important to clarify here that for the disciple of Jesus, wealth is not wrong. What is right or wrong is how the wealth is handled and if the wealth is treasured. In Job 31, Job is defending his righteousness. He has not withheld his riches from the poor, ignored widows and orphans, and stuffed his face while

---

[56] Caba presented this talk at the Justice Conference in Portland, OR in 2012.

others went hungry. He saw his wealth as serving the well-being of others not just himself. In verses 24-25 Job affirms that he has not put his trust and confidence in gold. He has not rejoiced in his wealth. His joy does not hang on it.

It would be easier for our consciences if wealth was just an individual thing and one was entitled to hoard all that they desired. It would have been easier for Job. But placing your joy in money is not just a personal spiritual problem—it is a shalom problem. It is a justice issue because it leads to the issues that Job is talking about earlier in the passage: withholding from the poor, not helping the widow, not warming those who have no clothes, and eating alone rather than with others who have nothing to eat.

Marshall passionately explains,

> It is not God's will that some should live in splendor and opulence while others starve and die. It is not God's will that some should hoard food and surplus land, while others languish in debt and servitude. This is why meeting the needs of the poor is not a matter of charity in the Bible, but an act of justice.[57]

Just as money is a morally neutral tool that may be used for good or for evil, for justice or for oppression—so it is with business.

My wife Melissa is always coming up with creative business ideas. Her parents have owned multiple businesses and she grew thinking in those terms. She's incredibly savvy with finances and has an entrepreneurial sprit. We're setting aside money so that eventually we can fund one of her business ideas. When we move forward with one of them, we'll want it to be something that is profitable. There is nothing wrong with that. What is right or wrong is how we run the business and what we do with the profit. The questions we need to ask ourselves are, "Is this giving others a window into God's Kingdom? Is this bringing about shalom through making things the way they ought to be in people's lives?"

---

[57] Marshall, 23.

Practically speaking, what does it look like to run a profitable business as mission? Keller says business owners "should not squeeze every penny of profit out of their businesses for themselves by charging the highest possible fees and prices to customers and paying the lowest possible wage to workers."[58] Instead they should honor workers and customers by not exploiting or taking advantage of them. They should relish helping people fulfill the cultural mandate and provide for their families by providing jobs.

Business owners should not do this for the sake of their business or their reputation, but for the glory of God and to create a better human community. As Michael Sandal points out in his lecture on Kantian ethics, to do the right thing for the wrong reason is not admirable. Such an action has no moral worth.[59]

Whether someone is a government leader, a church leader, or the head of their family they ought to participate in local justice work (Kingdom work) that addresses the complex causes that lead to poverty and injustice. They must grasp that both individuals and entire systems are corrupt and must be restored. After acknowledging that, either relief, development, or social reform must take place—whatever the situation calls for.[60]

KINGDOM CITIZENS ARE POLITICALLY AND SOCIALLY ENGAGED

Under first century Roman rule, there was a law which protected groups dedicated to the pursuit of a personal and spiri-

---

[58] Keller, 10.

[59] Michael Sandel. "Episode 06 - Justice with Michael Sandel." Harvard University's *Justice with Michael Sandel.*
http://www.justiceharvard.org/2011/02/episode-06/

[60] Keller, 113.

tual salvation. Members of who appealed to *cultus privatus* were never jailed, beaten, or martyred. Why did the early church fail to accept protection under this law?

Politics is "the regulation of the coexistence of human beings within a unit of rule, with a view to improving it in the present and in the future."[61] It is impossible to engage political dialogue without bringing one's personal values and ideology to the table. Political dialogue examines the dissonance between the way things are and the way things ought to be then attempts to pave a path forward. To say that the Kingdom of God brings some perspective to this discussion would be an enormous understatement!

How ought human beings live together? Folks of one political persuasion will rally around the ideal of freedom while advocates of a different system desire equality. Lesslie Newbigin suggests that God's vision is different than both freedom and equality and is the linchpin tenets for partisan politics.

"The Bible is informed by a vision of human nature for which neither freedom nor equality is fundamental; what is fundamental is relatedness. Man—man and female—is made for God in such a way that being in the image of God involves being bound together in this most profound of all mutual relations. . . . Human beings reach their true end in such relatedness, in bonds of mutual love and obedience that reflect the mutual relatedness in love that is the being of the Triune God himself."[62]

Throughout this book we have discussed the ideals of Scripture. And the ideal that governs God's Kingdom is love. Rightly ordered love is what allows humans to relate to God, others, self, and creation in harmonious fashion. And I have great news. Even if the President (or whoever else) doesn't hold to this truth, you and I can still live by this ideal!

Somehow, throughout history the Christian faith always seems most potent when it is on the fringes of society. During the third century under Constantine, Christianity became the

---

[61] Newbigin, 117.

[62] ibid, 118-19.

dominant religion. The emperor became a Christian and encouraged all to follow suite. Is that our highest hope for America? Perhaps for some it is. But I question how truly this vision meshes with Jesus' encouragement for us to be salt. Salt does its best work in modest quantities. Newbigin reminds us,

> Christians can live and bear witness under any regime, whatever its ideology. But Christians can never seek refuge in a ghetto where their faith is not proclaimed as public truth for all... Whatever the institutional relationship between the church and the state—and there are many possible relationships, no one of which is necessarily the right one for all times and places—the church can never cease to remind governments that they are under the rule of Christ and that he alone is the judge of all they do. The church can never accept the thesis that the central shrine of public life is empty."

With whatever voice the church has in whatever context the church finds itself, we are to use our voice to speak prophetically to the ruling powers and to help them identify what lies as the central shrine of public life. We are worshipping creatures. We have created government systems that help us worship our false loves.

The success story that drives capitalism is part truth, part myth, and part lie. The story of security and social equality that underlies socialism is part truth, part myth, part lie. The church must humbly and winsomely enter the public square and unveil these broken stories while proclaiming and embodying the true and better story of the Kingdom.

PARTICIPATING WITH GOD IN HIS KINGDOM

If we are to see what ought to be move forward in the name of Jesus, there are four significant keys to consider. Each is essential in seeing God glorified through his church and in our lives individually.

1. Believe some restoration is possible, and for that reason our work for justice is worth it.

In our world, we may be tempted to overlook present injustices for many reasons. We know that they are temporary and will be made right when Jesus returns. We may think someone else will take care of it. We may think we can't make much of a difference. But God paints a different picture for us through the prophet Isaiah.

Isaiah 58:12 is a gigantic promise, an immense vision, describing what God will bring about for people who align themselves with enacting God's will for the world—shalom. Isaiah talks about building foundations for future generations and rebuilding ancient ruins as well. The systems in the world that have fallen apart can be rebuilt by the power of the gospel. And the work the church does for the sake of the gospel right now lays down a foundation for future generations to build on. It might be tough to imagine what that can look like—but by his energizing Spirit, through the church, God is able to do immeasurably more than all we can ask or imagine.

2. Anticipate resistance from our flesh and those who prefer the status quo.

Obsession with security and comfort create great opposition to justice work both from within us and around us. This is not a new problem. People were just as selfish three hundred years ago, which is why Jonathan Edwards preached a sermon on "The Duty of Charity to the Poor" that still rings true today.[63]

Edwards anticipated the internal resistance people would have to the idea of doing justice and tackled those objections head on.

---

[63] Jonathan Edwards. "Christian Charity -- Johnathan Edwards." Bible Bulletin Board. accessed February 12, 2014. http://www.biblebb.com/files/edwards/charity.htm

- **Objection #1:** "They aren't too needy." Edwards responds by asking, "Would you want someone to wait to help you until you were at the end of your rope?"
- **Objection #2:** "I can't help anyone." Edwards replies, "What you probably mean is that you can't help anyone without burdening yourself and cutting into how you live your life. Yet, that is what the Bible asks of you."
- **Objection #3:** "They are undeserving and irresponsible." Edwards reminds us, "Have you heard of the grace of God? Given to undeserving, abusive, irresponsible people? Is that not our model? Furthermore, even if our charity will be abused it may serve as an example to those who see it, and a blessing to the children in the family who are victims of their parent's sin."

The biblical logic is certainly forceful in Edwards response to these common objections. The challenge he offers makes justice no longer an understanding issue—but an obedience issue.

3. Place equal focus on right belief (*orthodoxy*) and right practice (*orthopraxy*).

We must never be content to hear but not do. Personally, I'd rather know a lot less but do all of it than get really smart but not obey much. In an age of unprecedented access to information, it matters less and less what people know. What matters more and more are experiences. There is a level of knowledge and understanding that is only realized when we have participated and acted. Similarly, it could be argued that there is no *knowing* of God's will without actually doing it.

4. Find your corner of the Kingdom

My good friend Andrew is a pastor in Portland. Recently I brought a team from Adelphia down to his turf for a couple weeks to observe, learn, and serve. With a big smile, he welcomed us to the Montavilla neighborhood. We sat on colorful couches in the youth room as Andrew explained Portland and what we'd be seeing and experiencing throughout our time. As he talked about the teachers and students at the elementary school down the street he used people's first names. "This is my corner of the Kingdom," Andrew beamed.

There's a lot of talk about *world-changing*. It even shows up in the Jesus movie *Son of Man*. Early in the film Jesus is calling Peter. The scene plays out much like the biblical account. Peter says, "There won't be any fish." Jesus says, "Lay your nets here." Next thing you know the boat is bursting with a ridiculous catch of fish. Jesus says, "Follow me, Peter." Peter asks, "What are we going to do?" "Change the world," Jesus replies. In case you're wondering that last part isn't in the biblical text.

A few decades ago, every Disney channel show chronicled some junior high kid and the funny stuff that happened in their ordinary life. Pretty soon, those weren't the most popular shows anymore. A new breed of TV emerged. These shows were about famous kids like *Hannah Montana* and *Jett Jackson*. Nobody seemed to want to watch ordinary people anymore.

If the greatest affront to this generation is *being bored* then I would argue the close runner-up is *being unknown*. Everyone wants to be known, revered, and famous in their respective area.

But what if ordinary people are really the only kind of people? What if God is ok with ordinary people living life in their corners of the Kingdom?

Perhaps, you and I were made to live like Jesus in life's most simple moments. The Son of Man built stuff with wood in Nazareth for two decades. Perhaps, this is the kind of life Paul had in view when he said that we should seek to lead "a peaceful and quiet life, godly and dignified in every way" (2 Tm 2:2). If there is something in my soul that recoils at this prospect, what is that part of me?

If the most human experienced life the way it was intended to be by occupying one place (an obscure and impoverished town) and simply "being there"—what can that teach us about embracing the glamour-less moments and places we tend to despise in our lives? Only as the humanity of Jesus comes to shape my human life can I begin to find my corner of the Kingdom and participate in what God is already doing there.

THE INVITATION TO LIVE INTO A BETTER STORY

The world is messy. Many types of brokenness surround us— division, destruction, hatred, greed, slander, and debauchery. How does understanding God's desire for culture translate practically? Here are a few points for consideration and action.

- **What is?** Like a fish in water, it can be difficult to consciously observe the water we swim in. Yet Jesus and his disciples seemed to diligently observe people, places, and patterns that everyone else was gazing past. In the community you inhabit, what are the norms of life? What's good and enjoyable? What's broken or perverted?

- **What ought to be?** Disciples of Jesus are driven by a vision of a different kingdom. We know how God created things to be, how they were before the first sin. So ask the Spirit for some creative imagination and ponder: "What would this community look like if the Kingdom of God broke in? If Jesus was ruling here, what would be different?"

- **How can I participate?** What do you sense the Spirit asking you (and/or your church community) to create? Who or what is he asking you to confront? What specific actions and strategies will you enact to see the Kingdom of God break in?

Wherever you happen to find yourself right now, the surrounding culture is a landscape ravaged and twisted by sin yet still bearing glimmers of Eden. God is inviting you to participate with him in the renewal and restoration of all things. Under the leadership of Jesus, he invites you to make his invisible Kingdom visible. By the power of the Spirit, he invites you to abandon fear and imagine what ought to be and then pray, innovate, confront, create, redeem, and restore. It's time to live the true and better story that God is inviting us into.

THINK

- What "is" in your context?
- What ought to be?
- How can you participate in that vision individually and/or in community?

LOVE

- What kind of internal resistance is surfacing at the idea of participating in the Kingdom in this way?
- What fears are especially prominent for you as you consider finding your corner of the Kingdom?

DO

- Consider scheduling a half-day of silence and solitude for yourself. In a distraction free environment, listen to God and ask, "What's next?" Bring something to write down what you sense God is saying.

THE BEST STORY ALWAYS WINS
Conclusion

Lawyers sometimes have a saying they use when building their case behind closed doors: "The best story always wins." When it's time to render a verdict, the judge and the jury won't think about the information that was presented as much as they will be asking, "Which story is most compelling and coherent?"

Of course, you now know that the courtroom isn't the only place where story wars unfold. In the unseen corners of the human heart, story wars rage daily. These stories vie for supremacy on the silent channel of our thoughts. This battle is between the story of God and alternative broken stories.

TRUST THE BEST STORY

Actor Jim Carrey has famously said, "I wish everyone could get rich and famous and have everything they ever wanted so that they can see it's not the answer." Jim is saying, "Hey, wake up world. What you are chasing won't make you happy. That story is broken."

What if we took that advice? What if we allowed the Holy Spirit to begin to expose the emptiness of the stories we regularly trust in? How much more joy would we find in Jesus as we aligned ourselves with the true story of God? We would be free from lying successes, free from false loves, and free from broken stories. We would know the true story, trust the true story, and we would be set free to actually live a better story.

I can tell you that these ideas work with two-year olds. Parents, the beauty of grasping that sin is "loving the wrong things" is your toddler can understand it. I'm able to say things like, "Son, right now you are loving that toy more than your brother." That really drives at the heart. My encouragement to you is this: help your child see the story war in their own heart. What false loves can you help them identify? When they demand a toy forklift or a snow globe or a skateboard or an iPod or a candy bar you can ask them, "How long will these things make you happy for?"

THE STORY THAT NEVER RUNS OUT OF WORDS

Every book and every story runs out of words. In that moment, all we are left with is how those words re-shape our lives.

When John concludes his book on the life of Jesus he writes, "Now there are also many other things that Jesus did. Were every one of them to be written, I suppose that the world itself could not contain the books that would be written" (21:25).

Another way to express what John is saying is that the story of Jesus never runs out of words. Words fall short of capturing the beauty of his life on earth. Words can't capture the longevity of his life because he is eternal. Furthermore, God's story continues because his plans and purposes for our world are continuing to unfold.

Our lives are an opportunity to bring expression to the story of God. We've been invited to participate in this true and better story. It's the story that doesn't run out of words because God is still writing. He's writing in our lives right now as we submit to his Spirit and learn to love.

In our lives, in our families, in our churches, in our culture, may the best story win. The good news is, it will.

ACKNOWLEDGEMENTS

Six years ago my beautiful wife told me if I never wrote a book I would be missing part of God's design for my life. You were right Melissa. Thanks for running the show at home while I was in the office writing. Thanks for telling me when my ideas are worthy. I'm sorry for my over-the-top defensiveness when you tell me something doesn't make sense. You've supported me in every way possible. I love you.

Four years ago I joined an organization that has encouraged my lifelong pursuit of learning. To Rob and the Adelphia board, thank you for allowing me the freedom to press into my calling by studying, writing, and speaking beyond the bounds of my job description.

To Eric Tate, Jon Sweet, and Michael-Andrew Spalding: thank you for unleashing your creativity on this project. Your design, photography, and video skills have helped represent the essence of the book in a way I never could have accomplished on my own.

Two years ago I met Brad Watson. Brad invited me to write for GCD and has provided honest feedback for all the work I've done. Thanks for the opportunity Brad. It's been a joy to partner together. To Brad and the editing team at GCD, without your help this book wouldn't make sense.

A little over a year ago, Rick McKinley told me this manuscript was worthy of publication. Rick that small spark of encouragement gave me the courage to move ahead. Thank you for telling me that I have what it takes. Even more than that, thanks for pointing me to Jesus.

ABOUT THE AUTHOR

Sean (@Sean_Post) lives in Maple Valley, WA with his wife and two sons and leads a one-year discipleship experience for young adults called "Adelphia". He is completing his doctorate in Missional Leadership.

OTHER GCD RESOURCES

Visit GCDiscipleship.com

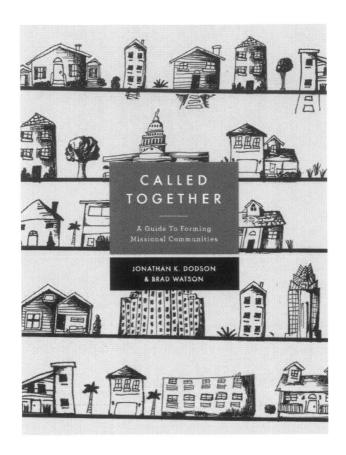

Everyone has a calling. We search for our calling in careers, hobbies, and even ministries, but Christians actually know their calling from birth. We are all called into God's community and onto his mission. There is no greater calling. Once we are in Christ, we are no longer orphans. Everyone has a place in the people of God. But how do you live out that calling? What does it look like to be God's new community? How can we fulfill our role in his mission?

Make, Mature, Multiply aims to help you become a disciple who truly understands the full joy of following Jesus. With a wide range of chapters from some of today's most battle-tested disciple-makers, this book is designed for any Christian seeking to know more about being a fully-formed disciple of Jesus who makes, matures, and multiplies fully-formed disciples of Jesus.

everPresent

HOW THE GOSPEL RELOCATES US IN THE PRESENT

By Jeremy Writebol

Foreword by Jonathan Dodson

"*everPresent* does something that most books don't achieve. Most focus either on who God is or what we should do. Jeremy starts with who God is to walk the reader down the path of what God has done, who we are because of God, then points us to understand what we do because of this. I highly recommend picking up *everPresent* to better understand the why and how of the life of those that follow Jesus."

SETH MCBEE

Executive Team Member, GCM Collective

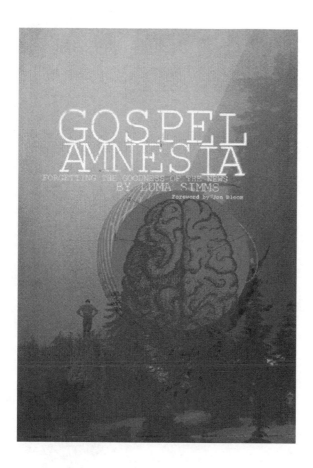

"Luma Simms remembers vividly what it was like to be simply going through the motions of a spiritual life. She writes like someone who has just been awakened from a nightmare and can still describe it in detail. Luma's voice communicates the pain of forgetting what matters most, and may be just the voice to reach the half-awake."

FRED SANDERS
Associate Professor of Theology,
Torrey Honors Institute, Biola University

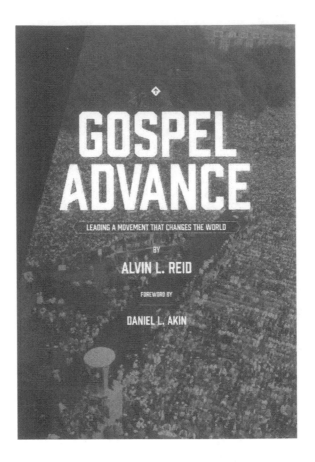

"*Gospel Advance* is Alvin Reid's challenge to the Church to re-
cover our mission focus and advance a movement of God
through the gospel. Reading this book is like sitting down across
from this passionate evangelism professor and hearing from his
heart. May the Lord use this work to ignite your heart for the
nations!"

TREVIN WAX
Managing Editor of The Gospel Project

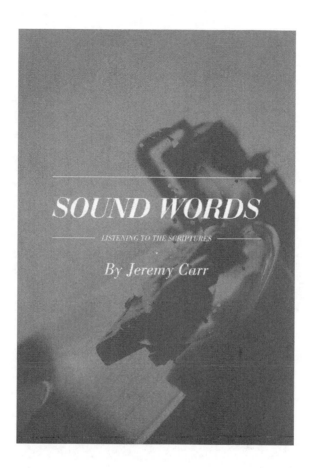

SOUND WORDS

LISTENING TO THE SCRIPTURES

By Jeremy Carr

"The church continues to need an understanding of discipleship that draws people to love and know God. This book delivers. It is an accessible and practical theology of scripture for discipleship. Jeremy is not exhorting you to love the Bible more, but declaring that God's love for you causes you to know and love him and his Word more."

JUSTIN S. HOLCOMB
Adjunct Professor of Theology and
Philosophy, Reformed Theological Seminary

Made in the USA
San Bernardino, CA
12 June 2015